# AFTER THE MASTERS

# Contemporary Indian Architecture
# AFTER THE MASTERS

Vikram Bhatt and Peter Scriver

Mapin Publishing Pvt. Ltd., Ahmedabad

# Acknowledgement

We would like to thank the following for their contributions of information and insight: Laurie Baker, Shirish Beri, Jai Rattan Bhalla, Ajoy Choudhury, Morad Chowdhury, Charles Correa, Ralino de Sousa, Balkrishna Doshi, Ashish Ganju, Jal Ghadiali, Satish Grover, Debasish Guha, Uttam Jain, Revathi and Vasant Kamath, Achyut Kanvinde, Sen Kapadia, Romi Khosla, Kamal Mangaldas, Hasmukh Patel, Nimish Patel, Leo Pereira, Poppo Pingel, Mahendra Raj, Anant and Amita Raje, Raj Rewal, Ranjit Sabikhi, Hema Sankalia, Jasbir and Saroj Sawhney, Kirtee Shah, Ram Sharma, Kuldip Singh, Namita and Satnam Singh, Joseph Allen Stein and Parul Zaveri. The time and resources of each of the above were willingly made available to us during the difficult but rewarding task of researching this book. In addition, we would like to thank the Center for Environmental Planning and Technology, Ahmedabad, for the use of their library.

We would also like to extend our appreciation to the staff and faculty of McGill University School of Architecture with whose assistance and encouragement we were able to produce the text. Particular thanks to Maureen Anderson, Julia Gersovitz and Charles Scriver for their editorial advice, and to friend and colleague Witold Rybczynski for his valuable and timely comments. Finally, special thanks are due to Razia Grover for her fine editing of our manuscript.

VB and PS.

First published in 1990 in the United States of America by Grantha Corporation, 80 Cliffedgeway, Middletown. NJ 07701 in association with Mapin Publishing Pvt. Ltd. Chidambaram, Ahmedabad 380 013 India.

Text and photographs © 1990 Vikram Bhatt and Peter Scriver except the following: Jain, U.C. p. 43 (bottom), 44-45 (center top, top right & bottom), 46-47,48,51, 52 Kapadia, Sen p. 208 (top) Patel, H.C. p. 36-37, 172-173 Raje, A.D. p. 76 (bottom), 77 (bottom), 199 (top and bottom), 200 (bottom), 202-203 (center top) Rewal, Raj p. 60, 61, 195, 196, 196-197 (center top) Sawhney, Jasbir p. 153 (bottom) Stein, Doshi, Bhalla p. 73 Thames & Hudson, *Le Corbusier* pp.90,103

ISBN 0-94-414219-2 ISBN 0-94-414253-2 (series) LC: 88-83653

Edited by Razia Grover Designed by Sunil Sen Drawings prepared by Jivan Patel from originals supplied by architects

Typeset in Century by Fotocomp Systems, Bombay Printed and bound by Tien Wah Press Pte. Ltd.

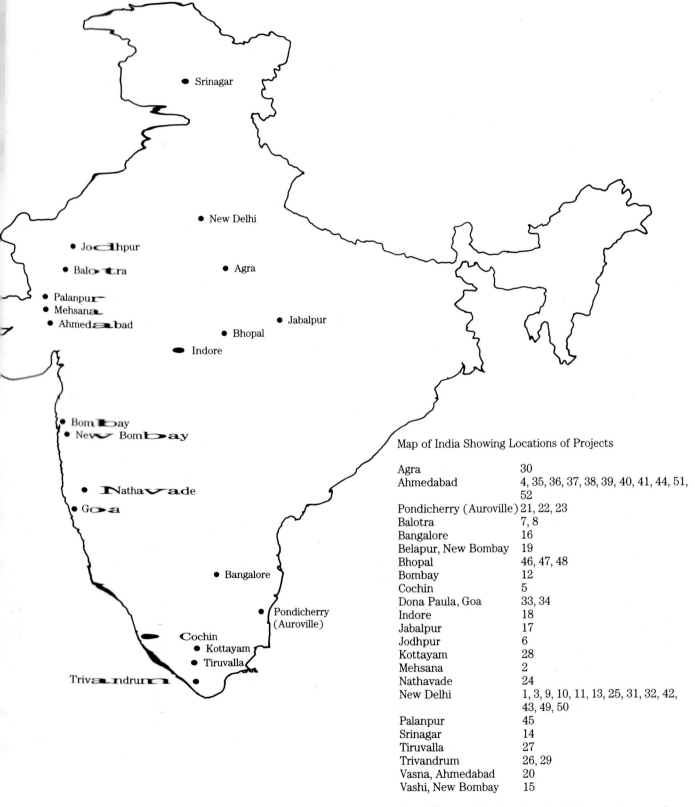

Map of India Showing Locations of Projects

| | |
|---|---|
| Agra | 30 |
| Ahmedabad | 4, 35, 36, 37, 38, 39, 40, 41, 44, 51, 52 |
| Pondicherry (Auroville) | 21, 22, 23 |
| Balotra | 7, 8 |
| Bangalore | 16 |
| Belapur, New Bombay | 19 |
| Bhopal | 46, 47, 48 |
| Bombay | 12 |
| Cochin | 5 |
| Dona Paula, Goa | 33, 34 |
| Indore | 18 |
| Jabalpur | 17 |
| Jodhpur | 6 |
| Kottayam | 28 |
| Mehsana | 2 |
| Nathavade | 24 |
| New Delhi | 1, 3, 9, 10, 11, 13, 25, 31, 32, 42, 43, 49, 50 |
| Palanpur | 45 |
| Srinagar | 14 |
| Tiruvalla | 27 |
| Trivandrum | 26, 29 |
| Vasna, Ahmedabad | 20 |
| Vashi, New Bombay | 15 |

Note: Figures following the city indicate project numbers

# Contents

# MAP OF INDIA

Map of India Showing Locations of Projects

| City | Project Numbers |
|------|-----------------|
| Agra | 30 |
| Ahmedabad | 4, 35, 36, 37, 38, 39, 40, 41, 44, 51, 52 |
| Pondicherry (Auroville) | 21, 22, 23 |
| Balotra | 7, 8 |
| Bangalore | 16 |
| Belapur, New Bombay | 19 |
| Bhopal | 46, 47, 48 |
| Bombay | 12 |
| Cochin | 5 |
| Dona Paula, Goa | 33, 34 |
| Indore | 18 |
| Jabalpur | 17 |
| Jodhpur | 6 |
| Kottayam | 28 |
| Mehsana | 2 |
| Nathavade | 24 |
| New Delhi | 1, 3, 9, 10, 11, 13, 25, 31, 32, 42, 43, 49, 50 |
| Palanpur | 45 |
| Srinagar | 14 |
| Tiruvalla | 27 |
| Trivandrum | 26, 29 |
| Vasna, Ahmedabad | 20 |
| Vashi, New Bombay | 15 |

Note: Figures following the city indicate project numbers

# Contents

# 1. INDIA: PROBLEMS AND PROSPECTS

"Why a book on contemporary Indian architecture?" one may ask. We have several good reasons, the most important being the country itself. India is both a land of ancient culture and a major society of the modern world. It is also the second most populous nation on earth. As with many developing countries, however, predominating issues such as poverty and overpopulation have precluded the appreciation of some fundamentally constructive processes. One such area of achievement is the work of India's architects.

India ranks amongst the largest construction markets in the world. Statistics for 1985 show that projects amounting to an estimated Rs. 400,000 million (about U.S. $ 30,000 million) were built or planned in that year.[1] While much of this construction is a response to rudimentary needs, the economy and clarity of intent with which such work must be undertaken can generate inspired and compelling architecture. How that derives and diverges from more universal tendencies in contemporary architecture is a question explored here.

Little has been published about design activity in the developing world. This discussion is a contribution to the thorough, region-by-region assessment of contemporary global architecture that is begging to be undertaken. It is our conviction that such an assessment would do much to renew the passion for the act and the art of building with which the current Architecture of Europe and North America has lost touch in its present state of complexity and confusion. The limitations of a developing economy can be a creative rather than an inhibiting constraint on architectural invention. In India, inspite of these limitations, works of immense significance have emerged. Examples better known to architects abroad include Le Corbusier's monumental government buildings at Chandigarh. In more recent Indian buildings of comparable scale and power, technical and economic limitations combine with a clear sense of purpose in the face of real needs to produce an architecture that has managed to elude the malaise and impotence of much current design in the West. It would be a mistake to confine an appraisal of this architecture within an exclusively Third World perspective.

Part of the challenge to practising architects in India is the dependence on a labour-intensive building industry. Mechanization and prefabrication do not yet compete on a cost-saving basis with the sheer abundance of manpower in India. Low-wage jobs in the construction industry are an important dynamic in the employment cycle of migrant labour from the countryside. Farming families, and sometimes entire communities move to the cities in the off-season to join the labour force on construction sites. Major operations, such as excavation, the mixing and pouring of concrete, and even the crushing of stone for aggregate and paving gravel are still carried out with simple tools and many hands. Donkeys and other animals are used to transport materials. Heavy mechanical equipment and large cranes are rare.

Technical backwardness is one facet of the remarkable presence of the past in modern India. Ritual, religion and living craft traditions descend from a cultural heritage of genius and beauty. These are perennial sources of inspiration to architects who attempt to embody identity and meaning in the design of new buildings. Skilled craftsmanship, high quality building stone and other traditional materials have been the abundant resources of the Indian architect since the time of the great temple builders. The building process today maintains an almost ritualistic link with that heritage. Despite the continuing commitment of many Indian architects to the image and functionalist planning principles of modern architecture, archaic techniques invest their buildings with a visceral quality of execution, at once youthful and timeless. Amidst the scepticism that pervades these closing years of the twentieth century, such architecture reaffirms the vernal promise of the early modern pioneers. Paradoxically, it also expresses that atavistic rationality of the 'hut in paradise' for which the pundits of post-industrial architectural theory have revived such a longing.[2]

Looking critically at the state of current design in India one challenges the notion of a 'regional' architecture. At a glance, the quest for a closer affinity to a physical and historical context is precisely what many interesting architects in India are engaged in but undoubtedly, any architecture that is competently and sensitively conceived responds intrinsically to its time and place. We are concerned that the directed pursuit of a regional style can impose a narrow perspective on architectural creativity. In the context of the developing countries, the appeal of an autonomous regional expression is all the more evident in the political and ideological game of symbols. The regionalist cause is intimately meshed with the notion of a Third World architecture. While a sense of solidarity in shared economic and social issues has inspired this idea of a special Third World identity, what that really entails is not apparent except that it excludes the forms of architectural expression that have come to symbolize the order and the values of the Western world. To adhere to such an artificial deduction is woefully simplistic — one must maintain an objective balance between perception and intention in architectural design.

Contemporary Indian architecture is a tangent of global architectural activity in the late twentieth century. It reflects many specific realities — some stimulating, some disturbing — of the environment in which it is conceived, but it is not the product of an isolated culture. Faith in the idea of growth and change remains the driving force of modern India along with most other societies of the world today. This ideal of progress transcends its Occidental origin. One no longer differentiates between East and West in the international order of communications, trade and technology by which even the most disparate nations manage to maintain some common ground. The contemporary architecture of India, as distinguished from the autonomous traditions of its ancient Buddhist and Hindu past, must be viewed in this context. It is the built expression of the socio-economic interaction between an interdependent global culture and the acute sense of place and past of India. The sources of design in these buildings are alien to the traditional culture; they reflect attitudes and techniques firmly rooted in the universal paradigm of modern architecture. It is through the process of design and construction that these sources are transformed and qualities of authenticity and originality are revealed in the best contemporary work.

Since the early 1970s Indian architects have emerged from the shadow of the many foreign masters — from the Persian designer of the Taj Mahal to America's Louis Kahn — who had dominated architectural design in the subcontinent. The present is characterized by a new confidence and new initiatives. Recent work reveals an effort to transcend the functionalist idiom in which so much of modern India has been built.

Fifty-two buildings and architectural projects have been documented in this book. Almost all have been designed since 1970 and some schemes are still under construction at the time of writing. The selection illustrates the wide range of tendencies and issues that have found expression in India's building efforts of the last two decades. Included are buildings of novel or polemical character along with the most distinguished examples of recent architecture. Our survey is only representative; many interesting buildings and architects have had to be overlooked. Our purpose has been to attempt an interpretation of the trends and intentions behind these projects. But the diversity of the architecture and the dramatically different realities to which it can be addressed, have made it difficult to view as a single process. Each of the four sections of the book is presented as an independent but parallel discussion of a particular facet of India's contemporary building activity supported by an appropriate selection of buildings and projects.

The first section concerns the elusive notion of an "Indian" architecture. This is a discussion on the continuing search for a relevant and evocative architectural expression. It is necessary to look back over the last half century for a better understanding of this abiding compulsion. We explore, in particular, the colonial beginnings of the architectural profession in India, and the influences of Le Corbusier and Louis Kahn on architectural design during the first two-and-a-half decades of political independence.

The second discussion concerns the inescapable issue of India's underdevelopment. The difficulties of designing and building in a developing economy affect all practising architects in India. Few, however, are professionally committed to the solution of the housing and environmental problems faced by the poorer masses. The relative handful of architects who are engaged in that process share a gut compulsion to help, but are motivated by a variety of different philosophies. The discussion of this small but important facet of Indian architecture revolves around their ideological debates. The question that emerges is fundamental: Does the architect have any role to play in the environment of the poor?

The opposing reality, the domain of most current architectural activity, is the marketplace of India's affluent middleclass. Here, we look at hotels, office buildings and exclusive housing projects; architecture that embodies the images of ambition and the nostalgic fantasies of an upwardly mobile society. While these buildings are frequently modelled on foreign precedents, the constraints of the developing context, historical imagery and popular taste can bring about some interesting transformations in the local product.

In the final section of this survey we resume the discussion of an Indian identity with a closer look at new design directions in the 1980s. This includes the work of a younger generation of architects who have been shaped by the theoretical debates of the 1970s. The finest work of the last few years reaffirms the validity of the Modernist paradigm even while architects respond to the Post-Modern call for more cultural introspection. The nature of these designs — institutions and complexes of an increasingly urban order — reflects the widening scope and significance of the architect's role in Indian society.

We have limited our discussion in this book to relatively few buildings so.as to delve more deeply into their interpretation: form, sources, intentions and meanings. There are, of course, inherent risks in any attempt to evaluate current work, and we do not presume to judge what will transcend the present, as great architecture must. In a developing context, such as India, the critic's criteria for judgement are especially uncertain as the process of change is capricious and multivalent in its cultural implications. Ultimately, there is not much purpose to a strictly evaluative .critique. It is more interesting, and more useful, to try to interpret why the different tendencies and attributes one observes have developed. Inevitably, one begins such an explanation of the present by looking at the past from which it has emerged.

The small existing literature on the architecture of India includes standard scholarly references that trace the evolution of the Hindu, Buddhist and Islamic traditions of building design. More recent additions to this historiography have attempted to appraise, for the first time, the two centuries of colonial architecture that bridge the period from the demise of the indigenous architectural canons to the present. However, the socio-cultural stigma of the 'colonial' still inhibits a dispassionate assessment of that British legacy. Until recently, it could not be discussed with any seriousness. However, the renewed respectability of the 'Raj' from the nostalgic perspective of current fashion, has encouraged an overly sentimental defence of the colonial building tradition. Fascination with the poetic tragedy of a lost Empire continues to hinder appreciation of the progressive phenomenon of British architecture and engineering in India. Barring the beginnings of a broader critical discourse in recent new journals and exhibition catalogues, only the Indian projects of Le Corbusier and Louis Kahn — important milestones in the history of modern architecture — have enjoyed any widespread exposure and critical discussion. Even then, they tend to be appreciated exclusive of their context. Existing criticism has not sufficiently emphasized the crucial inspiration of the Indian experience in both the design and realization of these major works.

Le Corbusier, Kahn, and the architecture of the British in India, are starting points for the present discussion. Our intention, is to interpret the ramifications of the colonial experience and the catalytic Modernist projects of the post-Independence era through examples of architecture built since the departure of those Western master-builders from the Indian scene. We have tried to maintain a critical distance in order to look at these buildings and their context at face value. Architecture is a universal activity. Although the conditions of architectural practice vary, and the possibilities for the stylization of architectural expression are unlimited, certain fundamental principles of design and building are common to all. One ought to be able to compare and discuss the work of all architects on this basis.

Our attempt at an impartial appraisal extends to the historical context from which the architectural expression of India is evolving. From our external perspective it appears that certain presumptions regarding the cultural history of India and its contacts with other cultures in the modern age, have introduced intriguing but possibly inappropriate dynamics into the development of its contemporary architectural expression. Our explanation for the present lies in a more accurate appreciation of both historical and temporal context — a global, rather than an ethno-centric reality.

**Notes:**

1. Gautam Bhatia, 'Building an Ugly and Ordinary India,' *The Times of India*, Section II, Habitat, 19 April 1986, New Delhi edition.
2. See Joseph Rykwert, *On Adam's House in Paradise*, Museum of Modern Art, New York, 1972.
3. See Shanti Jayawardene's perceptive critique of the confused collusion of 'regionalism' and the 'architecture of development' at a recent symposium on the topic; *MIMAR*, No. 25, Sept. 1987, pp. 77-80
4. William J.R. Curtis, Le Corbusier Ideas and Forms, Phaidon, London 1987.

# 2. ROOTS AND MODERNITY

A large Indian city such as Delhi is an architectural tableau of several different realities. There are extremes: imperial pomp and splendour on the one hand, and the marginal subsistence of rural migrants on the other. Framed between these is another picture; less poignant perhaps, but equally telling. This is composed of high-rise hotels, fly-overs and sports stadiums, acre upon acre of concrete domino houses, and the sprawling resettlement colonies of the urban fringe. It is the built expression of a young urban culture in the throes of rapid growth and transition. While these buildings express great expectations, they also reflect the traditions and the contemporary crises from which this emerging culture devolves. From its alien, Modernist origins the architecture appears to be moving towards a pre-industrial, even primitive, image that might be confidently labelled Indian.

Brash, exuberant, awkward, a striking illustration of this curiously Indian image of rough-and-ready technical potential is the complex of permanent exhibition halls built for the National Trade Fair in Delhi in 1972 (Fig. 2.1). This is not a refined or artful piece of construction, but its undisguised intent to project an image of modern India provides a provocative introduction to the quest for identity in recent Indian architecture. It also illustrates the paradox of this architecture and the society that builds it: a will to progress dependant upon the gangling manual energy of an over abundant work-force.

Fig. 2.1
Permanent Exhibition Structures, Raj Rewal, New Delhi.

The remarkable aspect of these structures lies in their reinforced concrete construction. Nowhere in the world have spaceframes of such considerable size been hand-built with rough formwork and manually poured concrete.

The design of this complex was commissioned on the basis of a competition. The winning submission had proposed a structural assembly of prefabricated elements in steel or concrete. However, the projected cost of this semi-industrialized process proved to be too high. Only by resorting to the crude facility of conventional labour-intensive construction methods could the structures be built within the available budget.[1] Ironically, what might have been a cliche of dated high-tech imagery became an inspiring statement by virtue of the almost absurd resourcefulness exhibited in its hand-hewn construction. The architect's willingness to compromise the intrinsic logic and prestige of his form source with the crude exuberance of the structures as actually built indicates the changing intentions in Indian architecture of the 1970s. Mere aspiration to the status quo was no longer adequate. Through the primitive building techniques that inhibited an accurate emulation of contemporary industrialized architectural production, the notion of a distinct identity for modern Indian architecture was beginning to find expression.[2] The exhibition structures display the new confidence and independence that have characterized the work of Indian architects from the early seventies to the present.

## MODERN LEGACIES

Contemporary Indian architecture has no formal roots in its own context. The compulsion to transform the alien modern idiom in the search for an Indian identity has been an impetus to the steady evolution of architectural design since the British era. However, the underlying principles of modern architecture have not been abandoned. An appreciation of this continuity of the Modernist paradigm in Indian culture — present and future — is essential in interpreting contemporary trends. It was the industrially based technology of steel reinforced concrete construction that provided the widely applicable principles on which a contemporary global architecture has developed. To create what might be called a regional expression is to make an appropriate fit of this universal doctrine to the conventional technology and imagination of a specific place and culture.

Recent Indian architecture has begun to show a certain autonomy in expression. However, the undisguised but discerning manipulation of the Modernist technique with which this special character is achieved, is evidence of the intimate initiation in the high Modernist tradition from which many contemporary Indian architects benefited in their early years. Whether or not a given architect had direct contact with prominent Western architects who were active on the Indian scene until the 1970s, the forms and images of his architecture derive, almost inevitably, from a Modernist conditioning.

In the early years of national independence, this stylistic dependency was lamented as the 'inferiority complex' of India's young architects.[3] It was hoped that a new architecture would revive the independent creative genius of classical India that have waned under colonialism. In the longer term, however, that proved to be a vain aspiration. The Modernist orientation of contemporary Indian architects was not only determined by training, but by the very nature of their profession in the new society for which they built. What appeared to be a revolution in architectural form and planning when the International Style began to replace the British colonial tradition of building in India, was really just a battle of style within the already established Modern paradigm. The socio-cultural revolution of modern India had begun long before the political transition of 1947.

## THE COLONIAL MODEL

Before the era of European rule, conquerors of the Indian subcontinent brought with them culture, government and sizable portions of their societies. Over the centuries these were absorbed and transformed by the existing culture. It is a deceit, however, to assume — as many do — that this pattern of assimilation has prevailed in the modern era.[4] The British consolidated their empire in India in an age when speed of communication and transport allowed the administrative and commercial arms of power to operate with a minimum of cultural and social intercourse. England remained a remote authority in politics, trade, and in the imperial culture that colonial architecture helped to promote.

The last phase of classical Indian architecture fell into decadence and eclecticism in the eighteenth century. Its demise was undoubtedly linked to the consolidation of European colonial interests in India during that time, although the degree of inculcation is debatable. British histories of Indian architecture did little to defend the case of the colonial intruders. Standard references such as Fergusson's of 1876 and Havell's of 1913 display an archaeological bias indifferent to the contemporary world. They are consistent, if unperceptive, in their repudiation of the new architecture and engineering that arose in British India and apparently eclipsed the genius of traditional Indian design. Those patronizing scholars failed to accept that intercourse with Europe had also brought about a fundamental expansion and transformation of the Indian culture. This new growth, rather than a cultural decline, was embodied in the architecture of the imperial age. As much in India, as throughout the Occidental world of the nineteenth century, the new public architecture — court houses, museums, legislatures and, of course, railway stations (Fig. 2.2) — was an integral expression of the cosmopolitan world-view of the new liberal societies emerging from the Industrial Revolution. The irony of it all was the paradox of colonialism. Underlying such magnificent symbols of Western faith in progress was a double standard for social development: one for the society of the conquerors, another for that of its subject races. Not unnaturally, this has hindered a dispassionate appreciation of colonial architecture in India.

The enthusiastic embrace of the language of the International Style, following Independence, quickly smothered the colonial tradition in Indian architecture. In the years ahead, the newly independent nation would, only slowly, realize the broad physical and social transformations heralded by her new architectural image. But a profound intellectual modernity had already been ingrained in middle-class Indian society as a result of the colonial experience.

Architecture, in the sense of a profession, was a foreign concept introduced to India by the British. The volume of construction actually designed by architects during the colonial era was however small. Then, as today, engineers and laymen in government service were awarded responsibility for the majority of public works. Private European architects whose expertise was largely directed to the building of opulent follies for wealthy princes. The few Indians who received formal architectural training in India before 1947, did so at the

Fig. 2.2
Howrah Bridge showing the steel structure.

*Opposite page*
Group of housing clusters (see p.60)     13

Fig. 2.3
Deco type building from Bombay.

Fig. 2.4
Central Secretariat, Herbert Baker, New Delhi.

Fig. 2.5
Revivalist building, Bhartiya Vidya Bhawan, Bombay.

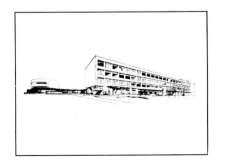

Fig. 2.6
Drawing of ATIRA, Ahmedabad, Kanvinde.

14

former Government School of Art in Bombay (the J.J. School of Art today). The Director, Claude Batley, was an Englishman who developed an active practice in India over many years. In his lectures, he maintained a pragmatic and essentially modern ideal of architecture: it was a universal craft, tailored rationally to regional parameters. Architecture in India, ". . . its origins, developments and decadence had followed the perfectly normal course of all the other world architectures and was inevitably based on the exigencies of local climate, building materials and social conditions . . . ."[6] An objective of Batley's course was to develop an informed appreciation of the similarities and the differences between the classical architectures of Europe and India. Students were required to do extensive field surveys of traditional Indian buildings to complement their theoretical grounding in the Graeco-Roman tradition.

In his own professional work — an obvious model for many of the young architects who trained under him — Batley tried to synthesize a style according to his belief in the parallel and compatible architectures of East and West. The resulting expression was progressive in the evolutionary sense of the term. It avoided the loud, revolutionary *éclat* of the machine-age imagery popular in contemporary Western architecture in favour of an archaeologically literate fusion of Western classical order with climatological principles and sculptural details from Indian building traditions. Only a handful of Batley's graduates, however, would carry on with this studied, assimilative notion of architectural style. Working primarily in Bombay, they produced a gamut of public buildings, commercial houses, cinemas and gracious upper-class residential developments in a refined but almost fanciful idiom that in the final analysis, owes more to art deco than to any continuing search for India (Fig. 2.3).

Edwin Lutyens' and Herbert Baker's buildings for the imperial government in New Delhi were the apex of the late-colonial style that Batley had tried to propagate (Fig. 2.4). But they were also the most obvious argument for the widespread rejection of that hybrid expression as the way to make architecture in an independent India. With their mandate to promote the image of the new nation, young architects in the 1940s and 1950s were keen for a revolutionary change and there was little question of carrying on as acolytes of the Raj.

Among the dissenters was a small but powerful camp of architects who advocated a determined revival of India's ancient architectural heritage. The principle enjoyed considerable popular and political support. In practice, however, the style tended to derive almost directly from Batley's hybrid design methods with a baroque predilection for Hindu and Saracenic garnish (Fig. 2.5). It had little to do with the true principles of ancient Indian architecture and more with a backward-looking affinity for British institutional planning. It was hardly inspiring. The dynamic and universal pretensions of the newest architecture from abroad were a timely repudiation of such cultural baggage. With the euphoric will to modernize that prevailed in India at the time of Independence, this contrived rendition of heritage was as readily rejected by the young cognoscenti of the architectural profession as was the British tradition.

With the demise of Mahatma Gandhi — and his intransigent resistance to the lure of modern technology — and Jawaharlal Nehru's subsequent assumption of full political leadership in 1948, the way was opened up for an Indian development policy modelled on the science and industry of the West. Through the 1950s, the building of the model city of Chandigarh would be the symbol of the Nehru era and the datum by which success would be measured. However, well before that showcase project — even in the British era — the Indian government had been sending young architects to the United States where they were exposed to the progressive imagery and techniques of the emerging International Style. Future doyens of the Indian architectural profession, such as Achyut Kanvinde who took his Master's degree under Walter Gropius at Harvard, returned home at the time of Independence to introduce this functional aesthetic through ambitious building programmes of the new government.

In 1947, Kanvinde was appointed Chief Architect for the Council of Scientific and Industrial Research. Over the next eight years he was responsible for the design and construction of several research laboratories and administrative complexes throughout the country (Fig. 2.6). These buildings were competent, straightforward renditions of the Bauhaus aesthetic by a young convert to Gropius' notions of architectural space defined by function and tailored to the expression of universal human values.

Nevertheless, enthusiasm for the International Style was already diminishing in India by the time Chandigarh's key monuments, with their seductive abstract forms, had been realized in the late 1950s. The sleek, white pastiche of the machine age was a less convincing embodiment of India's complex and paradoxical reality; the muddle of pre-industrial means and post-industrial ideals that has continued to characterize modern Indian society. Le Corbusier's late style was hardly more natural to India. However, it offered the Indian architect the model for a futuristic imagery that was ennobled by its responsiveness to the primitive circumstances in which it was conceived. It was a heroic strain of modern architecture for the developing world.

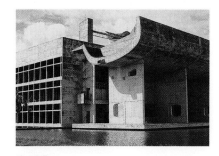

Fig. 2.7
Chandigarh Capital Complex.

## THE CHANDIGARH EXPERIENCE

The aging French master and the ambitions of the young Indian nation made for an odd but creative marriage in the design of Chandigarh. Le Corbusier had cultivated controversy throughout his career. In his work it was almost an ethic that creativity resulted from a struggle.[7] For Le Corbusier conflict was the quality essential to creative life, and the Indian experience generated plenty of it.

Le Corbusier was willingly drawn into heated controversy with the Revivalists. Their quest for an ethno-centric official architecture was best demonstrated in the planning and building style of Bhubaneshwara, the new capital city for the State of Orissa commissioned at the same time as Chandigarh. Le Corbusier's counter-attack was grounded in his notorious antagonism to the reactionary view of cultural tradition. The urbanistic principles to which he gave form at Chandigarh adhered closely to his long succession of unrealized projects for an ideal urban future. But the will to create was not satisfied with the mere restatement of previously formulated ideas. There was a stimulating new struggle inherent in his venture into India; the spiritual contest of an eccentric French intellect pitted against the stodginess of a lingering British-Indian mentality, and the intractable Eastern ways of thinking and seeing that colonial conditioning had concealed but not altered. This was expressed explicitly and originally in the isolated Capitol Complex that Le Corbusier designed as the symbolic 'head' of Chandigarh. His achievements in the planning of the city itself remain less certain. The master plan owes much to the preliminary studies of the American architects, Albert Mayer and Mathew Nowicki. In large part, the order and the architecture of the town as executed by Le Corbusier's principal collaborators, Pierre Jeanneret, Maxwell Fry and Jane Drew, is characterized by a democratic, self effacing banality. Le Corbusier's own architectural contributions exhibit no such doubts.[8]

Fig. 2.8
Curuchet's House, Argentina.

On a purely functional level, the semi-tropical plains of northern India presented a familiar challenge. The genesis of the building vocabulary used at Chandigarh can be seen in Le Corbusier's many schemes for North Africa and the handful of realized projects in South America and Mediterranean Europe. The Unité d'Habitations in Marseilles, the most significant antecedent to the Chandigarh project, was in the middle of construction when Le Corbusier made his first visit to India.

Le Corbusier's standard vocabulary for an architecture of heat and sunshine was the product of a rational analysis of climatological phenomena and building (Fig. 2.7). At Chandigarh, however, these elements were invested with a magnificent new quality of expression that appeared to derive line and figure from the forms of the Indian village. These were rendered in the crude *béton brut* (rough cast concrete) aesthetic that had first appeared in the Unité d'Habitation at Marseille.[9] But, in this regard also, the Indian experience provided truthful, naked inspiration for that previously missing expression. Throughout the prolific final decade of Le Corbusier's life, the spirit of his Indian projects would underscore the designs of such master-works as the Maisons Jaoul and the monastery of La Tourette.

The fecundity of Le Corbusier's Indian experience is even more evident when one compares Chandigarh, or even Le Corbusier's Ahmedabad buildings, with his contemporary projects in ostensibly similar regional contexts. It is interesting to observe, for example, that Le Corbusier's work in South America was not half as bold or intriguing in its formal expression. The house and clinic he built for a physician in La Plata, Argentina, during the early design stages of Chandigarh, is an ambiguous collage of his earlier style — the abstract play of pure forms — and tentative experiments with the emerging new expression of his final years (Fig. 2.8). It does not have the robust confidence of the Indian build-

Fig. 2.9
Akbar Hotel, Shiv Nath Prasad, New Delhi.

Fig. 2.10
Sarabhai House, Le Corbusier, Ahmedabad.

ings and suggests that the French architect was too close to home in that Latin cultural and intellectual milieu to find a fighting frame of reference for the creative struggle in which he thrived. Whereas Le Corbusier's ideals — his polemics of the earlier years in particular — had a considerable effect on the contemporary architecture of Latin America, he remained a remote inspiration in that continent. The projects he actually built in the region — the Argentinian commission, and his building for the Ministry of Education and Public Health in Rio de Janeiro (1937-42) — had comparatively negligible influence.[10] The probity of design and planning of the distant Indian projects appears to have made a greater impression. The trace of Chandigarh is obvious, for instance, in Lucio Costa's plan for Brasilia.

One observes little direct affinity between the contemporary architectures of the tropical developing nations. The influence of Le Corbusier's Indian projects is an exception, linked inescapably to the huge impact of the architect's ideas and buildings on the evolution of world architecture in this century. The prevailing colonial orientations of the developing world have tended to focus attention and admiration on European and American cultural sources, while a lateral view, towards alternative Third World sources, has been relatively unexplored.

In Latin America, a continuing sense of cultural union with the more developed western nations encouraged its architects to embark on an audacious and pluralistic exploration of Modernist architectural ideas as early as the 1920s. In India, by contrast, young architectural professionals were still isolated in the 1950s. Le Corbusier's direct and prolonged involvement in their forum was an enthralling experience that all but eclipsed influences from other quarters before the 1960s. It was an enviable collective apprenticeship, more immediate and applied than the type of exposure that most western architects could expect to gain from such a master. With Le Corbusier, and then again with Louis Kahn in the following decade, young Indian proteges got to observe, at first hand, the design process of the leading architects of the day. This experience demystified the ideals of architecture. It gave them tools to design their own buildings with audacity and skill.[11]

## EMULATION AND EVOLUTION

Literal emulation of Le Corbusier's late style has been an obvious tendency in Indian architectural design since the building of Chandigarh. Well into the seventies some of the finest architects in the country remained devoted to a Corbusian orthodoxy. Shiv Nath Prasad, a skilful designer in his own right, sublimated himself entirely in his veneration for Le Corbusier. His Akbar Hotel (New Delhi, 1965-69) is an impeccable fusion of the Unité d'Habitations and the Carpenter Arts Centre at Harvard (Fig. 2.9). The buildings of J.K. Choudhury for the Delhi campus of the Indian Institute of Technology (1961-84), and Rajinder Kumar's huge Interstate Bus Terminal designed for the New Delhi Municipal Corporation in 1969, evoke the monumental scale and sculptural abstractions of Chandigarh. They exhibit an almost religious faith in that expression as the archetype for public buildings in modern India.

But the mainstream of architectural practice in India has gradually evolved away from the Corbusian idiom. The process began, ironically, as early as the 1950s in the work of some of the ambitious young architects who had worked directly under Le Corbusier.

Among Le Corbusier's Indian followers, Balkrishna Doshi probably enjoyed the most intimate apprenticeship with the French master. After initial studies with Claude Batley in Bombay, Doshi journeyed to Europe to complete his practical training, joining Le Corbusier's Paris atelier in 1950. Four years later he returned to India to begin his own practice, while assisting in the supervision of four projects Le Corbusier's office had designed for wealthy industrialists and institution-builders in the city of Ahmedabad. One of these, the Sarabhai House, proved to be a watershed in Indian domestic architecture, one which would have a profound influence on Doshi's earliest efforts as an independent professional (Fig. 2.10). The house possessed a serene naturalism unprecedented in Le Corbusier's other Indian works and the contemporary architectural experience of his Indian followers. In fact, it was a revival of a vocabulary of naturalistic elements conceived much earlier: the rough masonry walls, shallow vaults and sod-covered roof Le Corbusier had used to build his arcadian divertissement of 1935, the *petit maison de weekend*, among several other unbuilt projects.

16

The impact of the Sarabhai House in India paralleled the excitement in Europe over the Maisons Jaoul, an intrinsically related design conceived by Le Corbusier at roughly the same time for a site in suburban Paris (Fig. 2.11). Both residential commissions brought the stylistic principles evolving in his current monumental projects back to the fundamental architectural test — the house. In these confident restatements of the archaic aesthetic of raw, economical materials friendly to man, he gave credence to a new ethic in modern architecture, effectively repudiating some of his own cherished ideals concerning appropriate form in the machine age.[12] Critical interest in the Maisons Jaoul, and the stylistic emulation of that building which pervaded architectural design in the West during the sixties, assured Indian architects that their parallel sympathy for the image and principles of the Sarabhai House was within the mainstream of global design thought.

While Balkrishna Doshi was overseeing the completion of Le Corbusier's Ahmedabad projects, the young architect started to receive some independent commissions. With these first opportunities to make his own architecture he began to explore and clarify an atavistic language of form and material descending from the Sarabhai and Jaoul houses. The minimalist aesthetic had arrived; a trend represented by the proliferation of the exposed brick and concrete bungalow with its decorative swatches of traditional textiles and terracotta figurines. Doshi and his contemporaries responded to this fashion with many variations on the new house type during the 1950s and 1960's.

Among the more significant works of Doshi's early career were his initial efforts to answer the housing needs of lower-income groups. The important groundwork that Pierre Jeanneret and Jane Drew had carried out on low-cost housing during the initial stages of Chandigarh, was furthered by Doshi in his Staff Housing for the Ahmedabad Textile Industries Research Association (ATIRA), built in 1956 (Fig. 2.12). The Chandigarh architects had experimented with the traditional uses of brick to make climatically effective housing solutions at a low cost. In the design of the ATIRA housing Doshi introduced a more timeless quality to the form of such dwellings. The link with the Sarabhai/Jaoul prototype was evident in the grace and simplicity of the shallow vault construction employed. Clusters of units were organized on principles derived from the settlement patterns of typical Indian villages. In this exercise, architecture was shown to be feasible for even the lowest-paid wage-earners.

The 1960s brought the first signals of a renewed evaluation and questioning of identity in Indian architecture. How well did the seductive new forms of modern design suit the reality of India?[13] Perturbed by this question, the tendency among followers of an original form-giver such as Le Corbusier, was to reduce and simplify the received style in order to transpose it to new applications. This tendency was revealed in Doshi's Lalbhai Dalpatbhai Institute of Indology (Ahmedabad, 1960). The imprint of Le Corbusier in this first institutional building by the young architect is clear. However, the characteristic Corbusian vocabulary is purged here of inappropriate idiosyncracies and some familiar elements are subtly transformed in form and proportion, to evoke the distinctive wooden vernacular of Gujarat. The building is contemporary, yet at one with the antiquities it enshrines.

Contemplative tranquillity qualifies another notable example of contemporary architectural design evoking values indigenous to India despite the alien precedents for its form. The Gandhi Smarak Sangrahalaya (Ahmedabad, 1960), a small memorial museum designed by Charles Correa, was among the architect's first commissions upon returning to India from his architectural studies in the U.S.A. (Fig. 2.13). It is a skilful synthesis of a foreign inspiration — Louis Kahn's Trenton Bath houses — with the humble materials used in the old ashram buildings adjacent to it, where the saintly father of the Indian nation lived with his community of followers for many years. The relationship between enclosed, in-between and open-to-sky spaces is the theme of this exercise in the subtle variations of a repeated order.

## KAHN IN INDIA

In 1962, the American architect, Louis Kahn, was invited to India to begin the design of a large campus for the Indian Institute of Management (IIM) at Ahmedabad (Fig. 2.14). Just as Chandigarh was to the 1950s, this ongoing project of the 1960s (along with Kahn's monumental designs for the eastern capital of

Fig. 2.11
Maisons Jaoul, Le Corbusier, Paris.

Fig. 2.12
ATIRA housing, Balkrishna Doshi, Ahmedabad.

Fig. 2.13
Gandhi Smarak Sangrahalaya, Charles Correa, Ahmedabad.

Fig. 2.14
IIM, Louis Kahn, Ahmedabad.

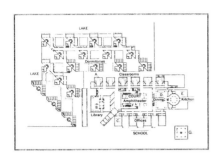

Fig. 2.15
Plan of IIM.

Fig. 2.16
IIT campus, Kanvinde, Kanpur.

Pakistan — now Bangladesh — at Dhaka) was an influential architectural intervention from abroad. In keeping with the experience of Le Corbusier and other foreign builders through Indian history, Kahn's work in the subcontinent encouraged significant evolution in his own design thought.

Kahn had a long standing love for brick ruins that was rekindled in India. He recognized a link between her ancient architectural glories and the surviving technologies of cottage-manufactured brick and labour-intensive construction. Such archaic practices went against the sophisticated construction systems used in his contemporary American work, such as the Richards Medical Research Laboratories in Philadelphia. In Ahmedabad, it gave him an excuse to build in brick on a scale that he could scarcely have imagined possible elsewhere. These buildings stretched the bounds of conventional masonry technology while they reaffirmed the timeless power of massive brick construction. Kahn's experiments helped promote brick to an almost exalted status in the vocabulary of the Indian architect.

The image of the Indian Institute of Management campus was a sober rebuttal to the heroic gesticulations of Le Corbusier's Chandigarh and Ahmedabad buildings. The urbanistic grouping of hostels and teaching blocks, with their arresting but austere geometry, offered a more stoic ideal of monumentality (Fig. 2.15). Here, in another highly personal statement, was an exploration of a universal vein of contemporary architecture that could, at the same time, lay claim to region and tradition.

Kahn's complete campus design was incrementally realized over the period of a decade, alongside the slow and politically complicated execution of his capital project at Dhaka. The influence of Kahn's architectural language was therefore delayed and would not be well expressed in the work of any Indian architect before the mid-1970s. While his work remained in progress, however, Kahn's professional and academic involvement with Balkrishna Doshi and his Ahmedabad colleagues, Anant Raje and Kulbhushan Jain, was an important inspiration for young architects training under those practitioners. It encouraged a new vein of building which gradually found its way into the form and principles of contemporary architectural design in India.

*

During the 1960s, the tendency to emulate the work of foreign architects did not diminish, but the sources of inspiration significantly diversified. More and more graduates from a growing number of professional schools of architecture in India were going abroad for further study in American and European schools. Returning home after a few years of practical experience in the West, these young architects were investigating a more plural perspective of the possibilities inherent in contemporary architecture. They would soon begin to discard the notion of a binding dogma, retaining only select details and principles from the legacies of Kahn, Le Corbusier and others for application in their work.

Hasmukh Patel, another productive architect from Ahmedabad, typifies this mainstream of the 1960s. Patel did graduate studies at Cornell University, which was outside the direct influence of the reigning American masters of the time. He apparently admired the work going on around him but maintained a critical distance. Back in India, this objective attitude to the styles and polemics of modern architecture was translated into deft though somewhat dispassionate design. One of Patel's earliest and finest buildings, a hostel for Jesuit priests completed in 1965, exhibits the skill of a methodical craftsman, drawing upon the obvious strengths of Kahn's and Le Corbusier's styles, delivering them in balanced measure in a crisply detailed building that is intimately suited to programme and climate. Patel and his contemporaries were eager to build and content to address the question of Indian context with a handful of proven materials and techniques.

Meanwhile, some of the first 'foreign-returned' architects to practise in India had already reached a stage of maturity as designers. Achyut Kanvinde was one. When Kahn was building the first phase of his IIM commission, Kanvinde had already built the seminal project of his early career, the Indian Institute of Technology at Kanpur (Fig. 2.16). For this extensive, multivalent institutional scheme, Kanvinde discarded the streamlined International Style of his first buildings in favour of an expressive assemblage of spatial and structural systems. Expressed concrete structure was the dynamic determinant of form and order in these buildings, although brick was almost as prominent. This sparse palette of materials encouraged a crisp, clean architectural expression similar in spirit to the detailing of Kahn's buildings, but without their monumental pretensions.

## BRUTALISM

Kanvinde's new expression clearly reflected the rise of the Brutalist polemic of modern architecture in the early 1960s. But curiously, he appeared to be committed to the *ethic* of Brutalism declared a decade earlier by Alison and Peter Smithson. He avoided the *aesthetic* with which Le Corbusier's Indian and European buildings in *béton brut* had seduced that movement away from theory, to become the relatively meaningless style so prevalent in new architecture around the world in that decade.[14]

For Kanvinde, the Brutalist ethic had renewed the promise of a modern architecture that could remain true to the cherished Functionalist notion, ". . . that the relationships of the parts and materials of a building are a working morality . . . ."[15] The new ethic advocated an architectural expression that was wilful and honest rather than aesthetically predetermined by the myths of the Modernist doctrine. It encouraged an aesthetic of vigour, derived from the violent conjunction of modern building materials, but it was committed in the last resort to a classical tradition rather than to any false or inappropriate technological paradigm.[16] It is ironic that many later buildings designed in this manner by Kanvinde's office are industrial facilities that herald the machine age that has still to reach much of the country.

During the design development stages of the Kanpur scheme, Achyut Kanvinde's office was a training ground for three talented young architects who had recently returned from work and study experiences in Europe and were at the height of their enthusiasm for Brutalist ideals. Morad Chowdhury, Ranjit Sabikhi and Ajoy Choudhury formed their own partnership in 1961 in Delhi as Design Group. Soon after, they began to make their mark with distinctive alternatives to the ersatz image of modern Indian housing that had become established since Independence. Several institutional schemes that they designed in the first half of the 1960s were innovative for their expressive articulation of individual units in low-rise group housing. Interestingly, this building-block expression anticipated the late Brutalist aesthetic popularized by Moshe Safdie's experimental housing project, Habitat, built for the World Fair of 1967 in Montreal. The similarity in image might have reflected a mutual knowledge of a still earlier precedent, Giancarlo de Carlo's student housing for the University of Urbino.[17] But the conscious intentions of both Safdie and Design Group to capture the character of vernacular townscapes found in hot dry climates is a more certain and interesting explanation. The peculiar stacking and street-like clustering of Design Group's housing evoked the built form of traditional North Indian cities. It was the precursor of a trend to assimilate contemporary architectural form to indigenous contexts that Design Group and other architects would actively promote in the 1970s.

Another important contribution to the image of Indian urban housing as it was evolving in the mid-1960s, was the work of Kuldip Singh for the Delhi Development Authority. At Usha Niketan, a small, middle-income, public-housing project of 1964, and in his much larger but conceptually related scheme at Saket begun a few years later, Singh used a strong mega-structural order to organize built form and infrastructure.[18] It was clearly distinct from the picturesque possibilities of Brutalism explored in the housing efforts of Design Group. But this repetitive determinism—with its rhythmic play of space and light and its three-dimensional weave of circulation and structure — also showed similarities to the spatial textures of old Indian cities.

## AFTER THE MASTERS

The year 1969 was the centenary of Mahatma Gandhi's birth. The event brought about a moral stock-taking by the planners and policy-makers of India. Where had the nation gone in twenty-two years of Independence and how had it stood up to the ideals of its founding father?

The fact was, India's development had followed quite a different course from that prescribed by Gandhi. His conservative ideals had served to unite the traditionally fractured communities of India in a collective bid for independence.

Fig. 2.17
Rajasthan vernacular.

But this solidarity was short-lived for, as V.S. Naipaul has argued, it was fostered as a 'racial sense' — a sense of belonging to a people specifically of the Indian subcontinent — that was ultimately too narrow and nationalistic to sustain credence.[19] Once freedom had been achieved, Gandhi's ethno-centric world view — especially his insistence on indigenous ingenuity and tradition — seemed to have lost its relevance for an ambitious new society that was anxious to join in the international game of modernization and progress.

Two decades later, India's burgeoning urban and industrial centres were evidence that much change had occurred. The architectural legacies of Louis Kahn, Le Corbusier and the many Indian architects they had inspired, were a distinctly non-Gandhian product of that initial period of big hopes and endeavour following Independence. It was apparent, however, that these signs of change described a development process that was capricious, often ineffectual, and sometimes destructive in the turbulence it caused. Meanwhile, the optimistic faith in a global community united in progress had faded rapidly in the clutch of the superpower politics that now dominated the post-colonial world. International uncertainty, Nehru's death in 1964 and border conflicts with neighbouring states, provoked a return to a more introspective world view. In the minds of many Indian intellectuals — architects and social activists among them — Gandhi's ideals once again presented a unifying wisdom for the time.

By 1969 the architectural profession had considerably matured. Indian architects began to look more confidently into their own milieu, conscious of their mandate to take up a more responsible role in the development of the country. The revival of Gandhi's call to build upon the indigenous technologies and symbols of Indian culture provided a moral basis for the rejection of the Western derived imagery of contemporary Indian architecture that had long been the concern of active thinkers in the profession. Since the late 1960s, architecture and other branches of design in India have accepted a conscious, and occasionally literal return to traditional order, form and craft as valid sources of imagery. In this regard, the constant challenge of urban housing has inspired interesting efforts. Also striking is the micro-regional identity that certain architects have been able to capture in powerful building contexts, such as the Himalayan foothills or the desert of Rajasthan.

## BACK TO ROOTS

The vernacular of Rajasthani desert towns such as Jodhpur or Jaisalmer, is among the most distinctive in India. Settlements in these arid regions are much like isolated island civilizations whose architecture has relied on strictly local sources for building material and inspiration. As a result, each town has its own unique image (Fig. 2.17). The common characteristic of this desert vernacular is a defiant exuberance in contrast to the austerity of the surrounding environment.

In his buildings for the University of Jodhpur, architect Uttam Jain used the yellow sandstone with which that city was built to make a sympathetic transformation of his own Brutalist design tendencies. A contemporary building type was planned with contemporary modernist principles of spatial organization. However, structure and form were determined according to the intrinsic order of load-bearing stone construction. Spans are therefore short; the buildings in general chunky and diminutive. Still, their mass and profile express the pride of classic desert architecture, while a flight of stone steps, or a narrow passage framed in stout masonry, evokes intimate experiences of the old town.

One of Uttam Jain's recent projects, a city hall for the desert town of Balotra, is a more complicated effort. It seeks to marry two rather different architectural types: the interior spatial order of a Jain temple and a contemporary Indian precedent for public architecture, the Legislature at Chandigarh. The building is, however, anything but an ode to these models. With its half-sized, toy-like *brise-soleil*, its black rubble-stone walls with their expressed white pointing, its mundane terrazzo and plaster interior finishes, and the folksy coloured glass doors admitting the tax-paying public into the cluttered two-storeyed forum within, it is an ironic essay on provincialism and popular culture in modern India. Together with Jain's Neelam Cinema built directly opposite, the building indicates interesting possibilities for an Indian post-modernism; a facet of contemporary architectural theory that has made only marginal inroads into the subcontinent to date. It suggests that the nature and nuances of a genuine regionalism — a sense of place — in architecture, are not to be isolated in a mere gloss of vernacular.

In the 1970s, urban housing was a focus of Indian architects' efforts to address the issue of identity in a developing society. Architects such as Ranjit Sabikhi and Ajoy Choudhury set about re-educating their clients to appreciate the high densities, social relationships and congested inward-looking spatial experience of traditional urban dwellings. By designing middle-class housing that forced some changes in lifestyle and a renewed sensibility for the Indianness of the environment, the space-seeking aspirations of the urban elite were subtly retrenched.

An interesting project of the mid-1970s was the Yamuna Housing Society in New Delhi by Design Group. This private residential colony for a community of South Indian civil servants was the somewhat rangy statement of a new prototype: low-rise contiguous built form defining internal semi-public *chowks* (small public open spaces) and pedestrian streets. In the Tara Apartments, a neighbouring development built about the same time by Charles Correa, a similar inward-looking street configuration was created. This was devised, ostensibly, to shelter a humid green zone within the development, but the building clearly shares the same typological basis as the Yamuna scheme. Both developments are schematics of traditional urban form. However, the dynamics of space use in the congested residential environments they emulate were not particularly well interpreted. In order to authenticate the traditional experience the detailing of the semi-public spaces within these developments needed to be less rigid in its stylistic determinism and perhaps more literal in its references to the vernacular.

In his design for the Athletes' Village for the Asian Games held in New Delhi in 1982, Raj Rewal went several steps closer to doing straight vernacular. The deliberate regional theme of the architecture was aimed as much at the higher-income residents who eventually moved into the project as it was intended to welcome the foreign athletes who were the initial users. Overt references to the architectural texture and built form of traditional townscapes in Rajasthan were the generator of an extensive residential complex that attempts to inspire identity and a compelling communal experience for conditioned suburbanites. Residents are invited to return to their humble roots in a fanciful realm of pedestrian streets and public spaces weaving through a fabric of low-rise sandstone coloured housing clusters. The rough, imperfect workmanship of this Public Works Department project was a reality the architect accounted for in his intentionally crude approach to detailing. This was played up as part of the return to basics. On the other hand, it is still an exclusive, modern housing project. Residents can drive their cars directly into their units and live a life of perfect privacy within spacious dwellings and adjoining terraces and gardens. This has created a dichotomy which is both quaint and convenient. However, this distinct layering of image and function does not amount to a progressive synthesis of contemporary and traditional orders.

Despite such overt image-making, Rewal's housing still exhibits the prevailing Brutalist tendencies of Indian architecture of the 1970s. Indeed, the evolution of that aesthetic into the mega-structural visions of the 1960s, and the isolated attempts in Canada, England and Japan to build a few such structures have been a recurring inspiration in Indian architecture into the present decade. Remarkable examples of this are several recent 'mega-buildings' by Raj Rewal, such as his State Trading Corporation office complex in New Delhi. This bears an uncanny resemblance to early Metabolist projects by Kenzo Tange and Arata Isozaki. Rewal's permanent exhibition halls of 1972, discussed at the beginning of this chapter, and the huge Marine Front Development in Cochin by Kuldip Singh, are other examples of this fascination with buildings conceived as huge, bombastic organisms.

A possible explanation for the prevailing popularity of Brutalism in the neo-Gandhian era of the 1970s was not the dynamism of that expression but its appropriateness from both a practical and a cultural point of view. As architects tried to look away from foreign form sources, they could regard the Brutalist aesthetic not as a heavy-handed version of modern architecture, but as a realistic and expressive product of India. It combined the rough materials and the manual processes of the Indian construction industry in an honest and potentially creative way. It was also apparent — as Kuldip Singh and Design Group had anticipated in their housing designs of the mid-1960s — that the style had some affinity with the brute morphology of vernacular architecture in various parts of India. However, the most convincing examples of this expression tended to avoid the risk of pastiche with a firm preference for a contemporary — sometimes heroic — pragmatism and image.

Charles Correa's Kanchenjunga apartment tower completed in 1983, is a strident, Brutalist-inspired building that strikes a challenging yet sympathetic chord of progress in the evolution of a contemporary Indian expression in architecture. It is a distinct contrast to the neo-medievalism of contemporary efforts in Delhi; a defiant last salute to Le Corbusier. The site of the Kanchenjunga tower is a landmark spot on the hilly lower western side of the Bombay peninsula. The building is Correa's bid at high profile image-making in a fiercely competitive real estate market; a jagged stack of sky- and breeze-seeking maisonettes that deliver an exciting new configuration for dwelling, and an euphoric symbol of the potential of architecture to change and possibly improve the shape of the environment.

## THE MODERNIST PARADIGM

Ultimately, it is an abiding faith in the basic Modernist doctrine that under-scores the most interesting individual tangents of architectural investigation and image-making in India today. The quest for identity is not abandoned in this work, but it is incorporated in an all-inclusive quest to evoke the identity of architecture itself — to build artfully in a given time and place.

Among the most enchanting examples of modern architecture to be found in India is the prestigious group of institutional buildings adjoining New Delhi's Lodi Gardens. This on-going project — a process of accretion, building by build-ing — has already spanned twenty-five years of the career of Joseph Allen Stein, an American architect long established in India. To date, the group comprises the offices and ancillary guest facilities of the Ford Foundation, UNICEF, the India International Centre, a gracious hostel and meeting facility for visiting academics and professionals. Two more institutions, the Indian headquarters of the World Wildlife Fund and a new secretariat for the Housing and Urban Development Corporation of India, are soon to be built. Stein's commitment to a consistent architectural image and the quality of his detailing in each addition to this scheme, illustrate the staying power of his Functionalist principles.

Stein's buildings stand outside any easy stylistic categorization with other contemporary Indian architecture. They are much in the spirit of the Internation-al Style. Yet, they accommodate their Indian context through intelligent detailing and a concern for the integration of built form and landscape. Conservation of the natural environment, a critical issue among India's overall development concerns, is the ethical preoccupation of this rather anti-urban architecture. The singularity of style can be traced to the architect's personal sources of experience outside India and again, quite possibly, to that curious impetus that the experience of designing in India has inspired in the work of architects from other cultures. Northern India has been an agreeable challenge to this Californian. His Lodi Estate buildings, with their meticulously rendered materials, perform handsome-ly in their semi-tropical setting. Transposed to the cooler climate of the Himalaya in his recently completed Kashmir Conference Centre, Stein's architecture is stripped clean of its sun-screening textures to emerge lean and elegant in the mountain light.

*

Some of the more eloquent examples of industrial architecture in recent years can be ascribed to Anant Raje, an Ahmedabad architect who worked for several years in close association with Louis Kahn. An illustration of the compell-ing vitality of modernism in Indian architecture is Raje's sprawling complex of warehouses and wholesale market facilities for the Maharashtra Agriculture and Food Corporation built near Bombay in the mid-1970s. There is a haunting monumentality that emanates from these pure volumes and surfaces in their multivalent, unrelenting order of relationships. It is Modernist industrial architecture, but devoid of either the mechanistic or the utilitarian expressions that are usually associated with such an ethic. One is reminded of the paintings of Giorgio de Chirico in which gaunt architectural vistas and pure form communi-cate such a profound, if surreal, sense of place. Raje's market halls possess timeless and intuitive qualities that transcend their function. They comprise a distinctly urbanistic composition that is uncannily similar to the architecture of the 'Tendenza' movement in Swiss Ticino and in the industrial north of Italy. The important influence of Louis Kahn on both Raje and the Italian neo-rationalists is a subliminal link between two architectural expressions that have little in common from a regional or formal point of view.

*

Balkrishna Doshi has evolved constantly through three prolific decades of commitment to both the practice and the teaching of architecture. His style cannot be specifically pinned down as each new commission brings forth new ideas and experiments. An exploration of spatial sequence and visual drama in an urbanistic interrelationship of parts is one of the more consistent formal investigations underlying Doshi's huge institutional projects of recent years: the Indian Institute of Management (IIM) at Bangalore, and the new administrative headquarters for the Madhya Pradesh Electricity Board at Jabalpur.

The imprint of Louis Kahn can once again be read in the 'particulate composition' of Doshi's plan for the I.I.M. campus, and the 'kissing squares' of the Jabalpur scheme, as Robert Stern has described these most characteristic and imitated idiosyncracies of the American master.[20] The spirit of the detailing of composite materials in each of these buildings hints enigmatically at Doshi's understanding of Kahn's architecture. In image these institutions are distinct from each other as they are in programme and regional locale. Their rationale is modernist, not historical in reference, yet they are experienced as architecture embodying the tradition and the power of the building. As the Jabalpur complex materializes on an ancient boulder-strewn ridge, it appears to extrude from the substance of the site, while it transforms the surrounding landscape with its determined profile. A fortress of the modern bureaucracy, it mirrors the palace-forts of feudal rulers only recently relegated to cultural memory.

## NOTES:

1. Ashok Lall, 'Trade Fair Exhibition Halls,' *Architecture + Design*, Jul-Aug 1985, p.29-37.
2. Ram Sharma, 'The Search For Roots And Relevance,' *Architecture In India*, Electa-Moniteur, Paris, 1985, p.112.
3. Claude Batley, quoted by Sharma, op. cit., p.112.
4. A.L. Basham, *The Wonder That Was India*, Fontana, London, 1971, p.489.
5. Edward Said has posed the challenging thesis that Western expert knowledge of the 'Orient' is a tradition of textual discourse comprised of a self-creating and self-legitimizing knowledge, intrinsically wed to relations of domination with regard to the East, See E. Said, Orientalism, Routledge and Kegan Paul, London, 1978.
6. Claude Batley, *Architecture*, Oxford Pamphlets On Indian Affairs, no.35, Bombay, 1946.
7. Charles Jencks, *Le Corbusier and the Tragic View of Architecture*, Harvard University Press, London, New York, 1973, p.179.
8. Sten Neilsson, *The New Capitals of India, Pakistan and Bangladesh*, Scandinavian Institute of Asian Studies, London, New York, 1973, p. 96.
9. Jencks. op. cit., p.142.
10. Henry-Russell Hitchcock, *Latin American Architecture Since 1945*, MOMA, London, New York, 1955, pp.11-13.
11. Malay Chatterjee, 'The Evolution of Contemporary Indian Architecture,' *Architecture in India*, Electa-Moniteur, Paris, 1985, p.132.
12. Reyner Banham, *The New Brutalism*, Reinhold, London, New York, 1966, pp.85-86.
13. Sharma, op. cit., p.112.
14. Banham, op. cit., p.85.
15. Ibid., p.135.
16. Jencks, op. cit., p.179.
17. Peter Serenyi, 'From Lutyens to Young Indian Architecture: Sixty Years of Housing in New Delhi,' *Techniques et Architecture*, Aug-Sept 1985, no.361, p. 58.
18. Ibid., p.59.
19. V.S. Naipaul, *India: A Wounded Civilization*, Penguin, New York, 1979, pp.154-155.
20. Robert Stern, *New Directions in American Architecture*, New York, 1969, pp.15-19.

## Permanent Exhibition Complex (Pragati Maidan) New Delhi

## Architect: Raj Rewal

## Client: The National Trade Fair Authority of India

Consultant: Mahendra Raj – Engineering Consultants India (structure)

Year of Completion: 1972

Area: Hall of Nations – 6,500 m$^2$; Halls of Industry – 8200 m$^2$

The 1972 Asian Trade Fair in Delhi was a national showcase marking the twenty-fifth year of India's Independence. The main exhibition complex, the focal point of the Fair, was the forum for the demonstration of India's industrial and technological potential. In view of the popular character of the project, a competition was held to select the design. The winning submission was selected for the clarity of its architectural statement and its inescapably dynamic structure, despite the difficulties this posed later in the execution of the project.

The structural principle employed to create the large column-free spaces required by the programme is the space frame. These particular structures are remarkable as they are constructed entirely of poured-in-place concrete. This labour intensive method, necessitated by the economics of the Indian building industry, has lent a distinctive hand-built identity to a structural type conventionally characterized by the delicacy and precision of prefabrication. A spindly octahedral lattice encloses the large crystalline volumes. Fenestration and sun breakers are incorporated in the 5-metre depth of the frame. The complex comprises five structures, four of which are fused together composing the Halls of Industry, each module spanning 40 metres. The larger Hall of Nations spans 78 metres. The halls enclose a public square with an amphitheatre between them.

1

2

1. Hall of Nations, corner entrance
2. Concrete spaceframe, detail
3. Hall of Industries, interior

*Overleaf*
4. Ceremonial entrance, Hall of Nations
5. Approach ramp, detail

3

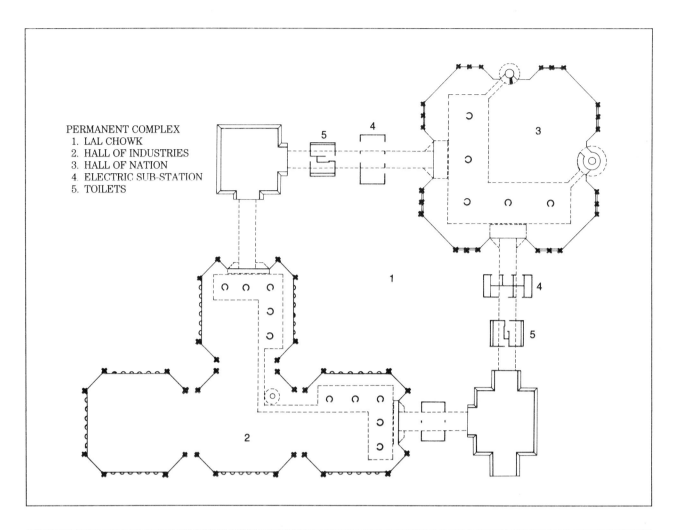

PERMANENT COMPLEX
1. LAL CHOWK
2. HALL OF INDUSTRIES
3. HALL OF NATION
4. ELECTRIC SUB-STATION
5. TOILETS

Dudhsagar Dairy Complex, Mehsana

Architect: Achyut Kanvinde –
Kanvinde Rai and Chowdhury

Client: Co-operative Milk Producers'
Union

Contractor: Parishram Builders

Consultant: V. S. Patel – Gannon Consulting
Services (structure)

Year of Completion: 1974

Area: 6000 m$^2$

In this large milk-processing facility, an anthropomorphic interpretation of building volumes — animal-like, if not expressly bovine — lends an unusually playful character to an industrial programme.

The principal high-rise element of the complex houses the dessicating process by which milk is made into powder. This, and the milk delivery and pasteurizing facility, adjoin an older dairy plant built several years earlier by another architect. The process of making milk powder, and the storing and shipping of the product determine the layout and hierarchy of structures in the complex. However, the architecture does not express the actual mechanics of production. Walls and structure are more theatrical than technical in their function of containing and supporting the process within. The milk condensing and spray drying equipment requires a multi-storeyed space. It also generates much excess heat that needs to be dissipated. The equipment is framed within a 7-metre square concrete grid that provides access to several levels. Metal grills permit air to pass from floor to floor around the periphery of each work space. On the exterior these ventilation points are expressed as large shafts that rise above the roof level. They evacuate the hot air by natural convection eliminating the need for a mechanical exhaust system. The difference in height between the spray drying and condensing facilities is aesthetically exploited to exaggerate a soaring mass and profile. Graphic banding of the exterior finish helps articulate the muscular physiognomy of the building.

1. Ventilating shafts, detail
2. Main processing plant
3. Milk delivery dock
   *Overleaf*
4. Expressive massing, shafts and central tower

1

2

3

29

4

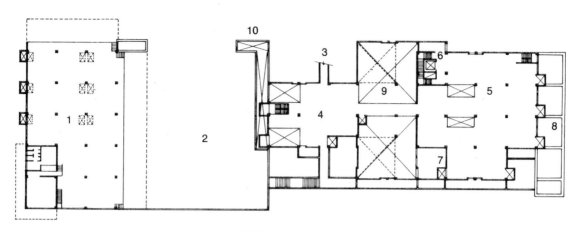

PLAN AT 112.5′

1. MILK RECEIVING
2. TRUCK DECK
3. ELEVATED DECK
4. TANKS
5. POWDER FILLING PACKING
6. GOODS LIFT
7. VENT SHAFT
8. CANOPY
9. SPRAY DRYER
10. SHAFT

1. MILK RECEIVING
2. SPRAY DRYER
3. VENT SHAFT

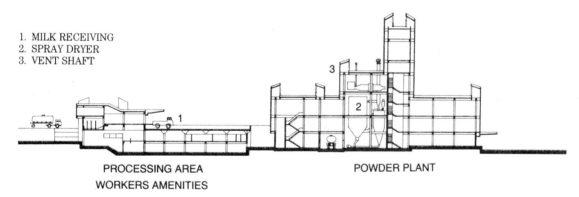

PROCESSING AREA
WORKERS AMENITIES

POWDER PLANT

SECTION

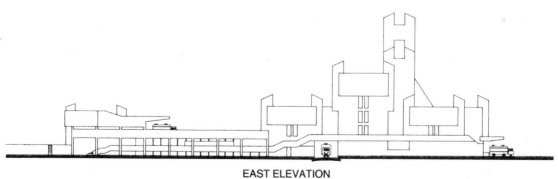

EAST ELEVATION

# National Dairy Development Board, Office Building, New Delhi

## Architect: Achyut Kanvinde – Kanvinde Rai and Chowdhury

## Client: National Dairy Development Board

Consultants: Mahendra Raj – Engineering Consultants India (structure)

Contractor: Gurubaksh Singh

Year of Completion: 1983

Area: 2700 m$^2$

With its irregular terracing and hanging roof gardens, this six-storeyed structure assumes a modest, almost domestic character befitting both its immediate residential surroundings and New Delhi's garden city character. The building is an alternative to conventional office planning in India. The socialistic emphasis on office-worker amenities and environmentally sensitive work space is reminiscent of Dutch architect Hermann Hertzberger's efforts in this vein. The client organization — a semi-governmental body responsible for some of India's most dynamic development programmes — has strong ties with Holland.

The building sets back from the street in receding, irregular terraces. Vertical services — fire escapes, main stairs and elevator towers — are concentrated at the rear of the structure as clearly expressed shafts. The pyramidal effect of terracing on the floor areas of upper storeys is appropriately exploited. More exclusive functions such as private offices for the chairman and director, and meeting rooms for the board and other committees are grouped at the top of the building. The larger, more public spaces, including the reception and the various departmental offices, comprise the lower floors. The exterior is finished with a rough plaster composed of marble chips and white cement; interior walls are plastered and whitewashed. Extensive built-in wooden shelving provides for storage of a large quantity of documents. The floors are of polished grey-green sandstone; terraces are paved with scrap pieces of the same stone. The quality of execution and finishes reflects the architect's attention to detailing and an experienced yet exploratory attitude to design.

1. Side elevation
2. Office terraces with hanging gardens

*Overleaf*
3. Front elevation, general view
4. Services and circulation concentrated at the back

4

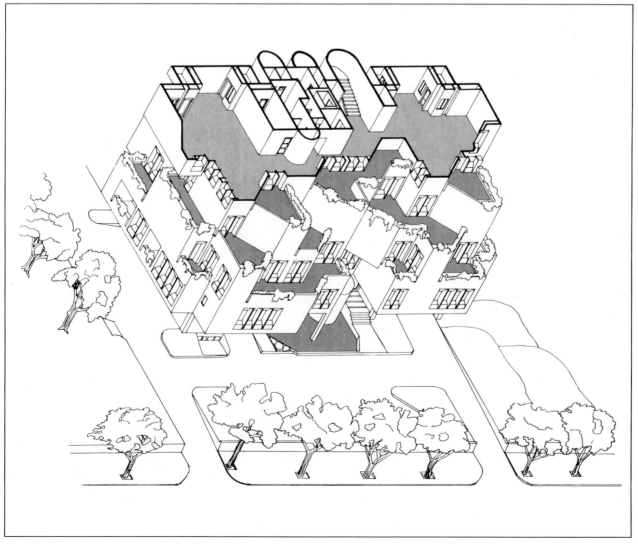

Newman Hall, Ahmedabad

Architect: Hasmukh C. Patel

Client: The Society of Jesus, Xaviers'
Kelavni Mandal

Consultants: Vakil-Mehta-Parikh-Sheth (structure)

Contractor: Reverend Brother Martin Araquistain
for the Society of Jesus

Year of Completion: 1965

Area: 3740 m$^2$

A clear and gracious order executed with
simple building techniques is the strength of this
design. For a residence for Jesuit seminarians, the
building is appropriately masculine in proportion,
and spare and explicit in every detail. In the
tradition of Jesuit missions around the world, it
declares itself with a confident but accommodating
catholicity. The assuredly modern, Cartesian order
of the building is graciously — and almost casually
— accommodated in the soft, subtropical
environment. Open corridors, articulated by the
rhythmic repetition of brick piers, are the essential
architectural experience of this contemplative
residential building. Medieval Christian cloisters of
Europe and the monastic austerity of Louis Kahn's
initial work in Ahmedabad are evident inspirations.

The three-storeyed structure is organized on
an H-shaped plan. Two blocks of individual cells
open on to common verandas that overlook an
inner quadrangle. A three-tiered bridge links the
two blocks to vertical circulation and a separate
common room. The chapel, a small free-standing
circular structure, is placed between the wings at
the top of the H. It completes the enclosure of the
quadrangle, a pleasant space casually planted with
shade-giving trees and bougainvillaea.

*Previous page*
1. Main facade

2. Verandah corridor adjoining individual cells
3. Chapel, central court

2

3

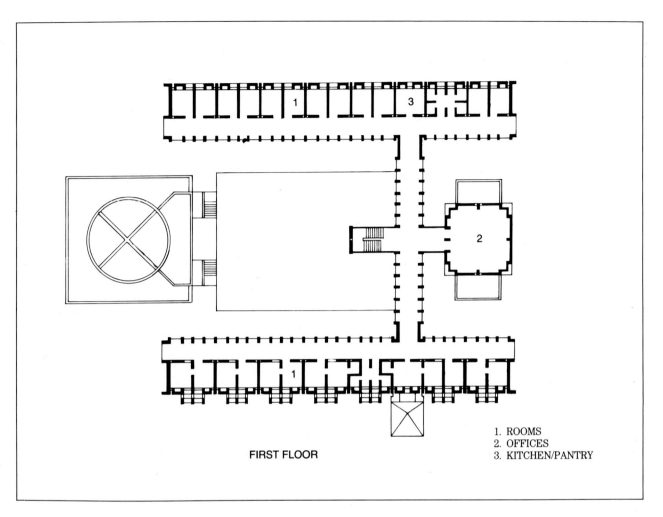

FIRST FLOOR

1. ROOMS
2. OFFICES
3. KITCHEN/PANTRY

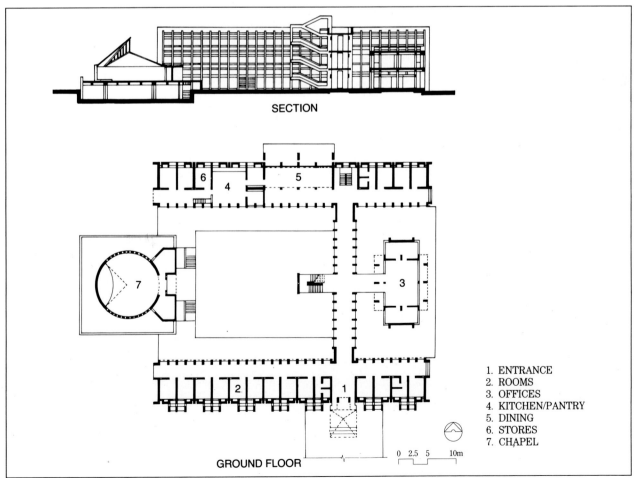

SECTION

GROUND FLOOR

1. ENTRANCE
2. ROOMS
3. OFFICES
4. KITCHEN/PANTRY
5. DINING
6. STORES
7. CHAPEL

0  2.5  5    10m

39

## Marine Front Housing, Cochin

## Architect: Kuldip Singh

## Client: Greater Cochin Urban Development Authority

Contractor: Cherian Verky

Consultant: ECI Engineering Consultants (India) Pvt. Ltd.

Year of Completion: 1984

Area: Phase I: 14,200 m², Phase II: 14204 m²

1. View from the harbour
2. Private terrace overlooking the harbour
3. General view

This multi-storeyed complex is part of a massive urban development project, the completed first stage of which includes two identical housing blocks with a commanding view of the ancient trading port of Cochin. It is a bold and unrestrained statement — typical of this architect's mega-structural persuasion. Each housing group is composed of a slab block terminated by a point tower. Most units are entered through single-loaded corridors concentrated on the east side of the block with the vertical services. The western exposure comprises private terraces overlooking the harbour. The slab buildings terrace back from the water as they rise. This is accentuated by the sloping party walls between terraces and the pointed gable roofs that crown the upper storeys. The large point towers also have chamfered tops and tiled roofs — an ironic gesture to the coastal vernacular which these giant buildings completely overpower.

2

3

# University of Jodhpur Campus, Jodhpur

## Architect: Uttam Jain

## Client: University of Jodhpur

Consultants: Shaman Engineering Company, C. M. Jain (structure); Technoconsultants (services)

Contractors: Rajasthan State Bridge and Construction Corporation Limited, Gordhanji and Company

Years of Completion: Lecture Theatre – 1971; Canteen and Arts and Social Sciences Block – 1985

Areas: Lecture Hall – 680 m$^2$; Canteen – 330 m$^2$; Arts and Social Science Block – 6970 m$^2$

This loose community of structures is given cohesiveness through the use of the golden-coloured sandstone with which the buildings of Jodhpur have been traditionally constructed. This stone serves as the primary building material and the determinant of the structural order of these contemporary yet contextual buildings. Steel and cement are used only minimally in this cost effective design and building approach. Walls are of dressed masonry laid in lime mortar; standard 3.5 metre-long stone slabs used as spanning members in floors and roofs determine the basic planning module. The university buildings are widely dispersed on the campus, but their sculptural expressiveness and their sun-etched stone textures make a strong imprint on the environment. Three buildings — the Faculty of Arts and Social Sciences, the Central Lecture Theatre cluster and the campus Canteen — standout among them.

The three wings of the Arts and Social Sciences complex form a U-shaped plan around a central open space. Internally, the classrooms, seminar rooms, laboratories and offices are organized along double-loaded corridors. A double-height courtyard with a surrounding colonnade, cross lighting at intervals, and the provision of wider areas in front of office clusters, animate what otherwise could have been a banal circulation scheme. To counter the hot, dry desert climate, the building is constructed with a double wall. The inner wall is structural with conventional glazed openings. The outer wall screens out direct sunlight. Its rhythmic openings follow the pattern of load-bearing stone piers behind. The sculptural gesture of the raised water tank and stair towers sandwiched between stone walls, and the ordered treatment of the facade give the building a bold presence.

The Lecture Theatre cluster is a small ziggurat-like structure mirroring the inclined seating in each of its four identical halls. Each is a simple rectangle in plan, supported by two parallel walls along its longer axis. These support the stone slab roof along with intermediate structural beams. A stone pergola screens the central node at which the four theatres emerge. An approach ramp, framed between two of the theatres recalls the sloping streets and soaring castle walls of Rajasthan's desert towns.

The Canteen comprises shared kitchen and service areas with separate dining facilities for staff and students. The staff area is a small mezzanine that overlooks the larger student dining hall below. It is reached by an open staircase rising from the entrance court. With its strong sculptural disposition, offset by a backdrop of rustic masonry, this staircase transforms the diminutive structure into a set-piece for some larger, still unfolding drama.

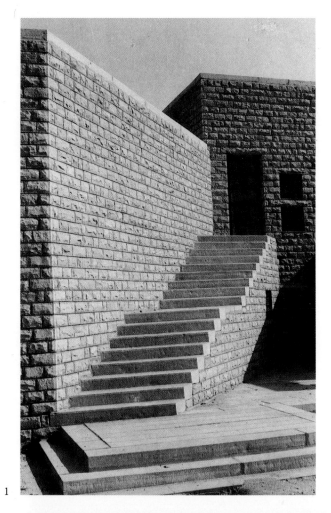

1. Entrance stair, staff canteen
2. Rhythmic progression of stone piers and towers, arts and social sciences block

   *Overleaf*
3. Lecture theatre cluster under construction
4. General view of arts and social sciences block
5. Access ramp, lecture theatre cluster
6. Trellised upper entrance space, lecture theatre cluster

1

2

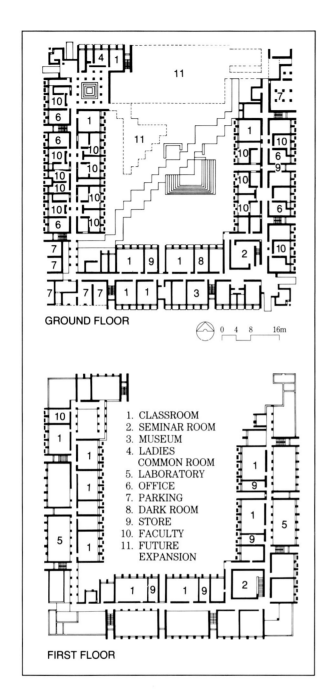

GROUND FLOOR

0 4 8 16m

1. CLASSROOM
2. SEMINAR ROOM
3. MUSEUM
4. LADIES
   COMMON ROOM
5. LABORATORY
6. OFFICE
7. PARKING
8. DARK ROOM
9. STORE
10. FACULTY
11. FUTURE
    EXPANSION

FIRST FLOOR

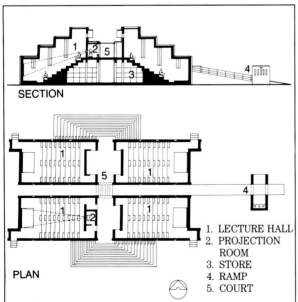

SECTION

PLAN

1. LECTURE HALL
2. PROJECTION
   ROOM
3. STORE
4. RAMP
5. COURT

3

4

44

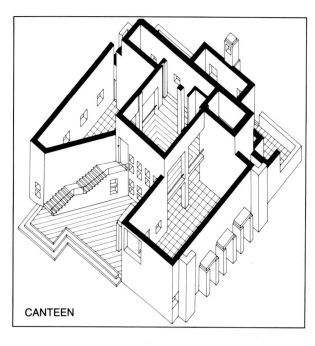

CANTEEN

5

6

Balotra City Hall, Balotra

Architect: Uttam Jain

Client: Balotra Municipal Council

Consultants: Shaman Engineering Company
(structure); Technoconsultants (services)

Contractor: Rajasthan State Bridge and
Construction Corporation Limited

Year of Completion: 1985

Area: 1994 m²

This proud but friendly piece of public
architecture is a popular treatment of the
expressive stone idiom the architect has evolved in
his buildings for the University of Jodhpur. The
building is a grand exercise for a small and
unassuming desert town. Sited on the highroad
leading into the bazaar, it is easily distinguished
from the banality of its surroundings by its formal
order. Yellow sandstone distinguishes the
monumental colonnade and screens of the longer
east and west facades of the rectangular block. The
autonomy of the building contained behind is
emphasized by the black rubble masonry of its
load-bearing walls. Polished terrazzo is applied to
most of the interior surfaces. Decorative detailing,
rendered in popular, almost folksy taste, softens
the official aura of the building. It includes varied
colours and patterns of terrazzo, coloured glass
windows and raised pointing on the exposed
masonry exterior. The architect has emphasized
public access with the oversized, double-height
entry hall that forms the heart of the building.
Although one questions the relevance of the
relationship, this space is intended to recall the
*mandapam* (sanctuary) of a Jain temple with its
distinctive cluster of columns rising in the centre of
the void.

The public hall serves as a reception foyer for
the mundane clerical functions that surround it on
three sides. A staircase ascends to an open
mezzanine and more offices above. The fourth side
is closed off by the wall of the council chamber, a
medium sized auditorium that will be available for
cultural events and public use when it is eventually
completed.

1

*Previous page*

1. Entrance hall

2. *Brise-soleil* screening rubble-stone facade
3. General view

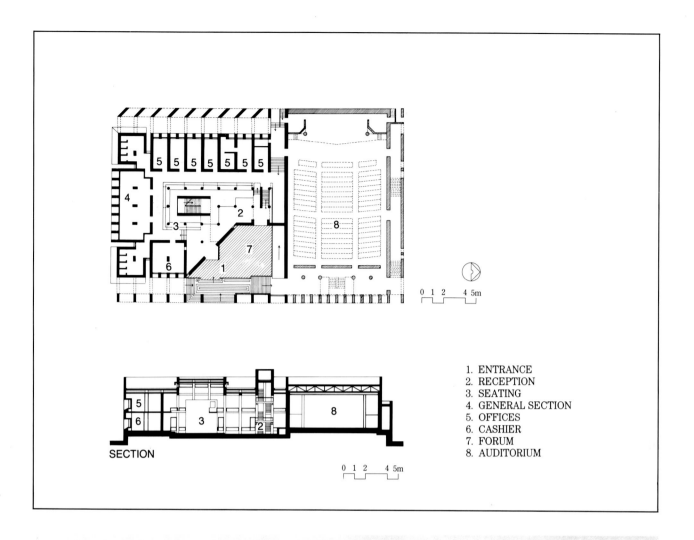

1. ENTRANCE
2. RECEPTION
3. SEATING
4. GENERAL SECTION
5. OFFICES
6. CASHIER
7. FORUM
8. AUDITORIUM

SECTION

## Neelam Cinema, Balotra

## Architect: Uttam Jain

## Client: Neelam Cinema

Consultants: Shaman Engineering Company
(structure)

Contractor: Departmental

Year of Completion: 1985

Area: 1980 m$^2$

The Neelam Cinema stands opposite the Balotra City Hall. Although this was an independent commercial commission, the architect has interpreted it as the cultural counterpoint to the public building across the road. The two designs gather between them an animate sense of place.

The cinema is a serious, if playful effort to make architecture out of a building type that rivals the temple for cultural significance in modern India — an awaking urban culture, eclectic in its tastes and imagery. The building is odd. Despite the straightforward simplicity of its lobby and auditorium, the elevations are unexpected — visual impact being an important aspect of the building's purpose. The architect has stretched his vernacular-conscious use of local building stone to new dimensions. The patterns and textures of the material as applied do not recall anything overtly colloquial, yet the hand of traditional builders is apparent. Their skilled but aesthetically naive technique is exploited by the architect to bring an anachronistic twist to contemporary commercialism. The building, a composite structure of steel and reinforced concrete, is enclosed with stone in a variety of rough and dressed textures. The patterns and chunky articulation that result are a provincial, vernacular variation on the graphic jazz usually associated with the chrome and plastic of urban cinema marquees. The corbelled fenestration of the lobby elevation is overshadowed by large apertures reserved for film posters. The whole facade has the larger-than-life aspect of a billboard. As one approaches Balotra from the desert, the exaggerated air-cooling exhaust grill that crowns the cinema is the only distinctive landmark visible; an ironic promise of civilization for the weary traveller.

1. Stone faced cinema marquee and ventilation tower
*Overleaf*
2. Master mason at work on elements for the facade

2

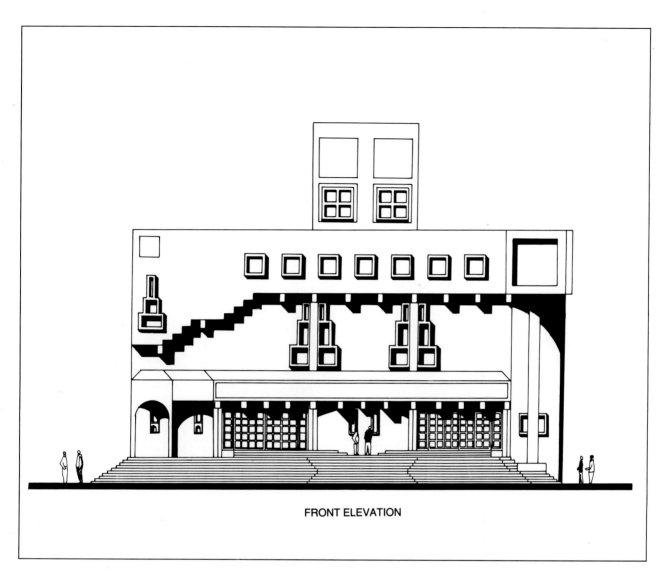

FRONT ELEVATION

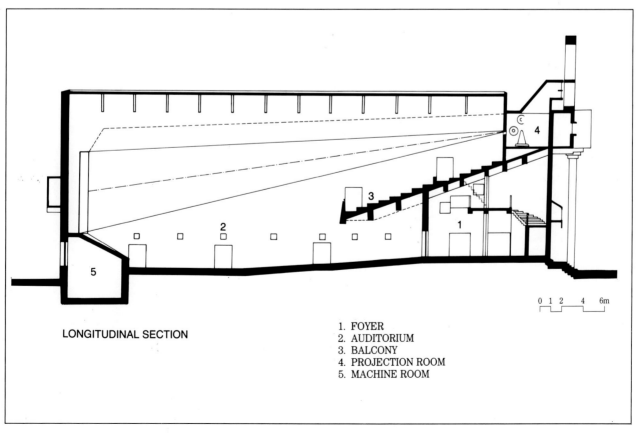

LONGITUDINAL SECTION

1. FOYER
2. AUDITORIUM
3. BALCONY
4. PROJECTION ROOM
5. MACHINE ROOM

0 1 2   4   6m

## Yamuna Housing, New Delhi

## Architect: Design Group

## Client: Yamuna Co-operative Group Housing Society

Consultant: T. S. Narayanswamy (structure)

Contractor: Departmental

Year of Completion: 1980

Area: 23,700 m² (200 units of varying sizes)

The designers of this low-rise, medium-density housing scheme produced intriguing reinterpretations of traditional built form in several earlier projects. This substantially larger scheme is a similar exercise, organized as a network of short and narrow pedestrian streets that approximate the scale and texture of the older residential quarters of many Indian cities. The gesture is, however, ambiguous. The explicit expression of material and structure once favoured under the banner of Brutalism has been subdued here with a chalky veneer of aggregate plaster, and token arches are punched through veranda partitions. An image of rather aggressive modernity prevails, nonetheless. A limited range of unit types leads to an inevitable repetition of standard volumes and details. The particularly heavy-handed massing alludes to a crude masonry vernacular but achieves a different expression as a result of this regimental determinism.

The development was designed for a group of civil servants of South Indian origin. Particular religious requirements specific to their orthodox Hindu lifestyle were observed in the planning of the living units. For example, a special prayer room has been designed to adjoin the kitchen area of each dwelling. The compact clustering and pedestrian orientation of the buildings, and the homogeneity of the user group has produced a strong sense of community. A grassy common and a hard-surfaced public space with a stage for outdoor performances, are integrated into the scheme. Unfortunately, security requirements and a ring of peripheral parking have caused the buildings to be set in a compound removed from the street and neighbouring housing projects, which has compromised the urbanistic *parti* of this complex.

1

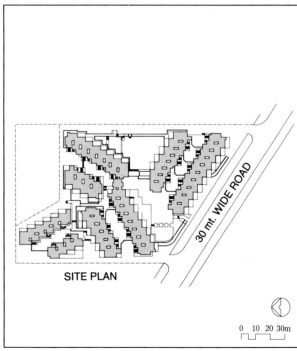

SITE PLAN

30 mt. WIDE ROAD

0 10 20 30m

1. Private gardens adjoining ground floor units. Terraces and balconies of overhanging upper units.
2. Interior pedestrian street

Tara Group Housing, New Delhi

Architect: Charles Correa
Jasbir Sawhney (associate architect)
Landscape Architect: Ravindra Bhan

Client: Tara Co-operative Housing
Society

Consultants: Mahendra Raj – Engineering
Consultants India (structure)

Contractor: Ahluwalia Construction Company

Year of Completion: 1978

Area: 160 maisonettes varying in size from 84 m$^2$ to
130 m$^2$

The street-like organization of this low-rise
high density housing development (160 units on a
0.8 hectare site) reflects a return to vernacular
form sources that became popular in Indian
housing efforts of the 1970s. However, this *parti*
derives specifically from the climatological rationale
of the narrow overhung streets in desert towns
such as Jaisalmer. Literal quotation of traditional
form or details has been avoided. The unusually
refined exposed brick and concrete construction
reflects the architect's prevailing commitment to
the Modernist idiom.

The internal streetscape is interpreted as a
shady garden, informally landscaped with trees and
water to enhance humidity. It is terraced to fit the
topographic profile of the site. This irregular
contour is echoed in the staggered rows of housing
that frame the space and in the terraced set-backs
of the external elevations. Living units are
two-storeyed maisonettes, 3 metres wide and 15
metres long, each clearly expressed in the
articulated mass of the building. Lower units are
accessible at grade from the internal street; upper
units are reached by common stairs. These units
open out onto private roof terraces framed by a
giant concrete pergola that serves as a cornice to
the composition. This characteristic device is
somewhat vestigial in Correa's application of it
here. It accentuates the jagged breakdown of the
building's surfaces rather than forming an effective,
continuous parasol.

1.  Landscaping, interior court

    *Overleaf*
2.  Access stairs and entrance balconies overlooking interior court
3.  Exterior view

2

3

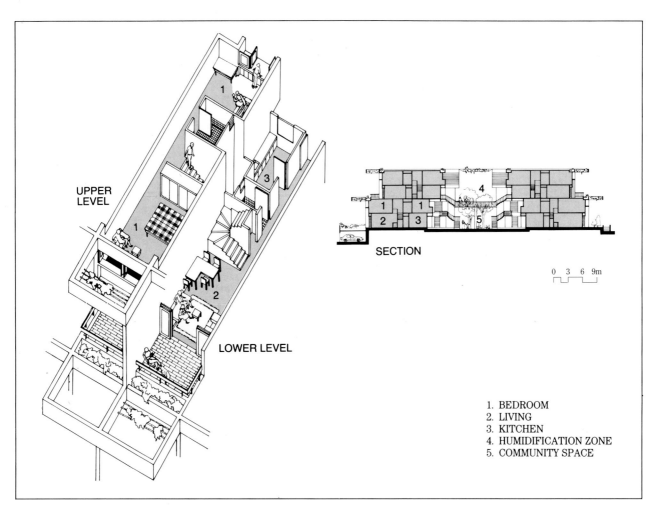

UPPER LEVEL

1

LOWER LEVEL

SECTION

3

2

4

5

0   3   6  9m

1. BEDROOM
2. LIVING
3. KITCHEN
4. HUMIDIFICATION ZONE
5. COMMUNITY SPACE

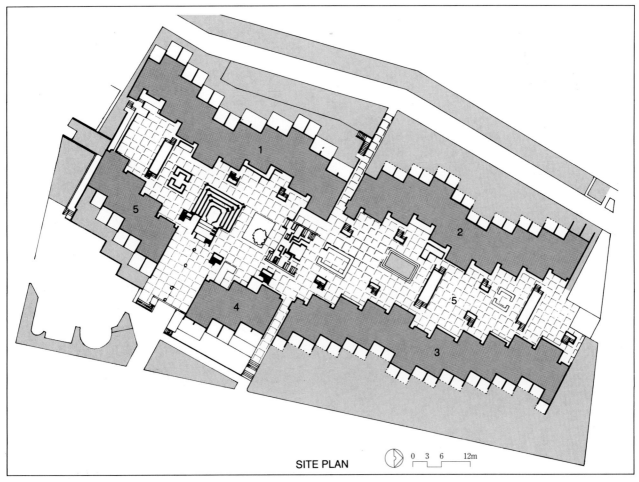

SITE PLAN

0   3   6      12m

59

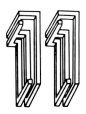

Asiad Village, New Delhi

Architect: Raj Rewal

Landscape Architect: Mohammed
Shaheer

Client: Delhi Development Authority

Consultant: N. F. Patel Associates (structure)

Contractors: Anant Raj Agencies with Jeevan
Builders and Bindra Builders

Year of Completion: 1982

Area: 700 units varying in size from 90 m$^2$ to
200 m$^2$

1

This sizable housing development was created as a short-term accommodation for athletes attending the 1982 Asian Games held in New Delhi. The vernacular character of the scheme was intended to communicate a sense of place to visiting competitors in that international event. It was also conceived as public housing, the function to which the project reverted following the Games, albeit for higher-income tenants. The commission for the Village was awarded through a design competition, with only two years lead time in which to complete the 700 unit project. The winning architect chose to exploit the rough and ready quality of construction that one would inevitably have to accept in order to realize such a rush project. This has determined the image and form of the housing. A traditional urban fabric of *mohallas* (narrow pedestrian alleys), gateways and courtyards is suggested in the blocking and clustering of the housing. The architect avoids

pastiche, however, by abstracting the gesture to a somewhat mechanical game of patterns and geometry.

The basis of organization is a neighbourhood group of twelve to thirty-six units, organized around a common space. Clusters are interlinked by a series of gateways framed by overhanging housing units. The basic cluster is a flexible composition that can be added to or multiplied in several different ways. The privacy of terraces in individual units is maintained with parapet walls, perforated to allow air to circulate. This is an important consideration as the terraces are used for outdoor sleeping during the hot summer months. The housing is finished with a coat of cement mortar pargetted with yellow sandstone aggregate. These wall surfaces are broken down into expressed panels resembling slabs of stone, lending a more domestic scale to the complex.

3

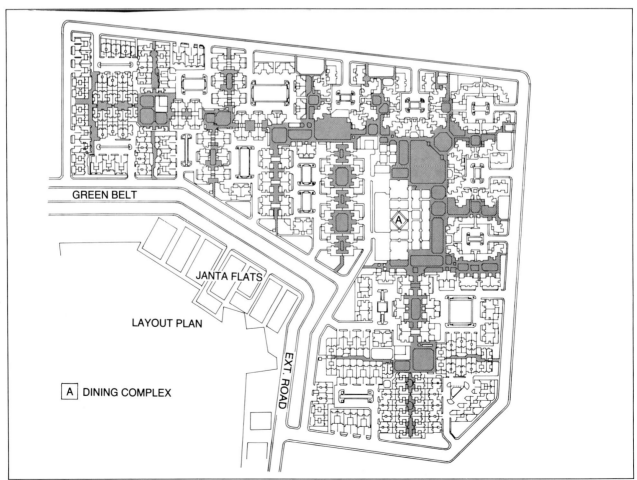

GREEN BELT

JANTA FLATS

LAYOUT PLAN

A  DINING COMPLEX

EXT ROAD

*Previous page*
1. Group of housing clusters forming a *chowk*
2. Pedestrian street linking several *chowks*

3. Cluster of housing units
4. Garden entrance to typical unit

4

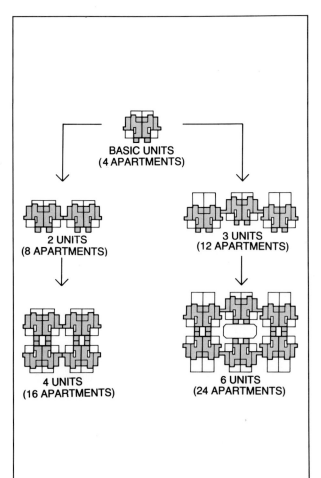

BASIC UNITS
(4 APARTMENTS)

2 UNITS
(8 APARTMENTS)

3 UNITS
(12 APARTMENTS)

4 UNITS
(16 APARTMENTS)

6 UNITS
(24 APARTMENTS)

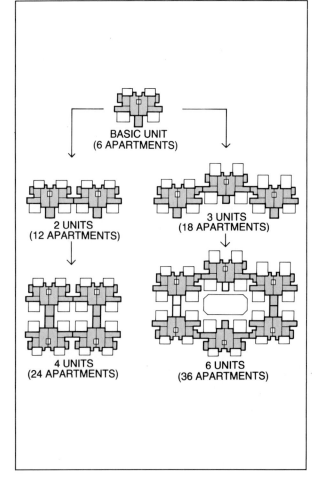

BASIC UNIT
(6 APARTMENTS)

2 UNITS
(12 APARTMENTS)

3 UNITS
(18 APARTMENTS)

4 UNITS
(24 APARTMENTS)

6 UNITS
(36 APARTMENTS)

## Kanchenjunga Apartments, Bombay

### Architect: Charles Correa;
Pravina Mehta (associate architect)

### Client: T.V. Patel

Consultants: Shrish Patel Associates (structure)

Contractor: Engineering Construction Company

Year of Completion: 1983

Area: 32 apartments varying in size from 180 m$^2$ to 420 m$^2$

The Kanchenjunga building is an exclusive housing development. With spectacular views of both the Bombay skyline and the Arabian Sea, it exploits a tiny parcel of prime urban real estate to the utmost. The tower is a fusion of efficient point-block circulation and commodious maisonette housing commonly applied in low- and medium-rise slab blocks. Skip-stop elevators give access to a jagged stack of split-level units, each of which rises and descends from the central core to double-height verandas nicked out of the corners of the building. These large outdoor rooms protect the principal living spaces from direct sun and serve as wind-catchers to enhance natural ventilation. The resulting articulation of an otherwise simple extrusion of concrete — enhanced by the distinctive, irregular perforation of the shear walls by small square windows — is reminiscent of the formal transformations of the cube that Le Corbusier explored in his design for the Shodhan Villa (Ahmedabad, 1954). Varied, vibrant tones and patterns of coloured tiles applied to the inset walls of the terrace spaces, give a distinctive identity to individual units. Small balconies overlook the private terrace spaces, creating an intimate domestic scale within the giant order of the building.

1

1. Corner detail
2. Apartment tower, general view

   *Overleaf*
3. Balconies and breeze seeking corner loggias
4. Corner loggia, detail

4

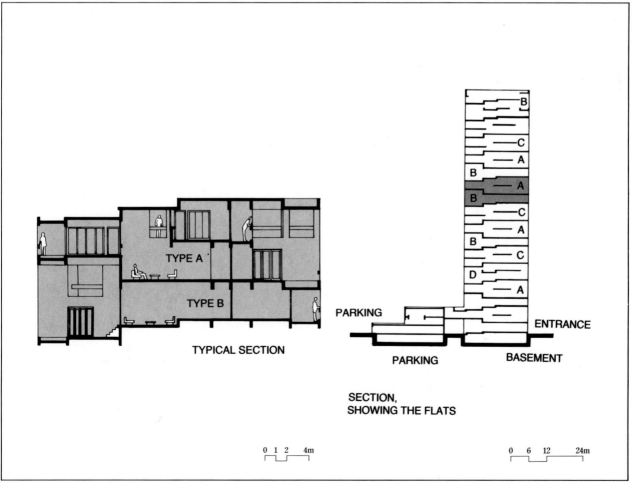

TYPE A

TYPE B

TYPICAL SECTION

0 1 2    4m

PARKING

PARKING

ENTRANCE

BASEMENT

SECTION,
SHOWING THE FLATS

0  6  12    24m

B
C
A
B
A
B
C
A
B
C
D
A

67

## Lodi Estate Institutional Group, New Delhi

### Architect: Joseph Allen Stein

### Clients: India International Centre, The Ford Foundation

Contractors: Northern Construction Company, Tirath Ram Ahuja and Baldev Nagrath

Year of Completion: 1962 (Phase I)

Areas: India International Centre – 6000 m$^2$; Ford Foundation – 5000 m$^2$ and UNICEF – 4000 m$^2$

This collection of institutional buildings is the cumulative product of almost three decades of slow and fastidious development. Each element is a variation on the rich, romantic strain of Modernism achieved in the design of the first phase of the development, the India International Centre, completed in 1962. The architecture renews, in modern internationalist guise, an attitude to design much closer to eastern tradition — and in that regard, more universal — than those European strains of Modernism introduced to India by Le Corbusier and the Bauhaus tradition. The American architect, a long-term resident and practitioner in India, had apprenticed with Richard Neutra at the start of his career. Still earlier, he had studied under Eliel Saarinen, the Finnish master of early Modern design and craft. These influences are revealed in a meticulously designed ensemble that coalesces casually from well-crafted elements and details. The form and concept of the buildings are governed by principles but no finite typology. Growth and evolution are graciously accommodated.

The India International Centre is a combined guest house, cultural centre and social club. Members are a cosmopolitan mix of academics, professionals and artists for whom the centre provides a retreat from the affairs and grittier realities of the capital city. The architecture strikes a subtle balance between contextual and technical appropriateness on the one hand, and on the other, modern standards for space organization, amenities and services comforting to foreign visitors. This balance rests on the choice of simple durable materials and their explicit detailing. Concrete — exceptionally well-finished — is the basis of the structure. A cast *in situ* concrete frame supports precast roof and floor elements, carefully devised for each of the major space types: auditorium, lounges, dining room, guest rooms, and small office and seminar spaces in the programme block. Local grey stone is used extensively in bearing walls. A delicately crafted *jali* (lattice of brick that diffuses light and admits breeze) protects all the window exposures from direct sunlight. In an innovative reinterpretation of the traditional device, small tiles and tubular aluminum spacers are used to compose this curtain. The *jali* reduces thermal loads on air-conditioned portions of the building while tying together the porous breakdown of building elements behind its elegant sweep. The informal but carefully choreographed displacement of the building's various blocks and elements serves to incorporate the intensively landscaped site in the architectural experience. The picturesque interplay between buildings and gardens reflects the architect's respect for the fifteenth century Lodi Tombs and public gardens that align the site.

The later buildings for several independent institutions have observed much the same spirit. However, each possesses its own character. The Ford Foundation, now occupied by the United Nations Development Programme, was built in 1968. It is a vigorously articulated building. Open bridges and pergolas link the loose composition around irregular garden courts with fountains and reflective pools. Stone walls and expressed concrete structure, capped with a flying horizontal cornice, comprise the masculine physiognomy of this building. The solid piers and floating horizontal floors with their weeping planters, recall the architecture of Wright and Neutra. But the hermetic air-conditioned enclosure of the building unfortunately interrupts the flow of space from the building interiors to the garden.

More recent additions to the group include a science centre for the Council of Scientific and Industrial Research, completed in 1972, the Indian headquarters for UNICEF, completed in 1981, and offices for the World Wildlife Fund, currently under construction. Recently, the architect was invited to devise a set of architectural guidelines by means of which municipal authorities plan to control and harmonize extensive new institutional developments slated for this prestigious garden city sector of New Delhi.

1. Ford Foundation/UNDP, detail
2. India International Centre, entrance court facade

*Overleaf*
3. Ford Foundation/UNDP, general view
4. India International Centre, guest room wing
5. Offices for UNICEF
6. *Jali* detail

1

2

3

4

5

6

# Kashmir Conference Centre, Srinagar

## Architect: Joseph Allen Stein – Stein Doshi and Bhalla

## Client: Government of Jammu and Kashmir

Consultants: Mahendra Raj – Engineering Consultants India (structure)

Contractor: Amarnath Charanji Lal

Year of Completion: 1984

Area: N/A

The Himalayan vale of Kashmir, a celebrated beauty spot of India, is suffering considerable ecological strain from unchecked tourism-related development. The major project, to build an international conference facility and a 325-room hotel, posed a potentially destructive threat to the environment. The architects, therefore, turned to the formal Mughal gardens of Kashmir as a guideline for a sensitive intervention in this enchanted natural setting.

The complex sits on an auspicious point of land projecting into Dal Lake. This site was selected to avoid marring the landscape with a large hillside development. However, the building is an inevitable imposition, even among the tall poplars of the lakeside. Wisely, the architecture does not pretend to disappear; it engages the landscape in a formal dialogue by which the natural and man-made environments are harmoniously integrated. Extensive glazing and a delicately trabeated concrete structure, suitable in the mild alpine climate, lend the buildings a cool transparency uncommon in the architecture of the Indian plains. Terraced gardens and formal reflecting pools, descending to the glassy sheet of the lake and snow-capped mountains beyond, extend the architecture into the landscape.

The building resolves into three functional zones. Long-span spaces comprise the conference facility at the eastern end of the complex. A network of courtyards formed by single-loaded blocks of guest rooms is the other anchor of the composition. The lobby, lounges and restaurants are grouped in between on the axis of entry.

The structure is broken down into regular blocks. Large double-height spaces are supported with heavy beams and H-shaped columns in a tartan grid. A secondary structure encloses these volumes with elegantly proportioned wood and concrete fenestration that echoes the main structural grid. Masonry infill is rendered on the exterior with precast concrete block of a distinctive greenish hue textured with a decorative pattern in relief. Less successful details include the sloping slate roofs, an unconvincing attempt to harmonize the building profile with colloquial built form and the landscape. Inside, the heavy-handed structure of the large lobby spaces results in some awkward and inefficient conditions; a failing redeemed, however, by the eloquent detailing of other chambers, such as the principal auditorium with its exceptional wood finishes. This space is also graced with a fine tapestry, an example of the extensive furnishings and textiles designed specially for the Conference Centre by the architect and his project team.

1.  Entrance hall, conference centre

    *Overleaf*
2.  Arrival court, hotel
3.  Finish detail
4.  Gabled guest wings
5.  Interior court, hotel
6.  View of Lake Dal from garden terrace
7.  General view from the gardens

2

3

4

5

6

7

# Semi-Wholesale Market, Vashi, New Bombay

## Architect: Anant Raje

## Client: Maharashtra Agriculture and Fertilizer Corporation Limited

Consultant: Sharad R. Shah (structure)

Contractor: Nirdip Construction

Year of Completion: 1975

Area: 8800 m$^2$

Only the first phase of this regional wholesale market has been built. For political reasons, even this portion of the scheme is unused. Already in a state of decay, it is, however, a rare building that transcends functional obsolesence with the significance of its architectural design.

Explicit hierarchies of structural form and building functions lend organization to a sprawling complex. Specific space types give identity to each activity — the farmers' warehouses, the main auction hall and the farmers' market. The low-rise complex is urban in concept and experience. Alley-like passages vaulted by concrete shells emerge on narrow streets which open, in turn, on to squares meant for gatherings. The farmers' warehouses are grouped in long ranks, each has an office, a storage space and a sleeping loft with an attached washroom. The auction hall is a large vaulted canopy divided in two distinct parts by an inclined incision in the roof volume. It floats above an open platform which can be readily reached by delivery trucks. The general market halls are organized for the semi-wholesale distribution of produce purchased at the auction. Smaller offices overlook these spaces from an upper level. A spartan palate of materials — cement-faced masonry with vaults and roofs surfaced with scintillating white china mosaic — emphasizes the severe simplicity of the forms employed.

1. View of internal street from market hall
2. Auction hall
3. Model, overall facility
4. Vault detail, auction hall

1

2

3

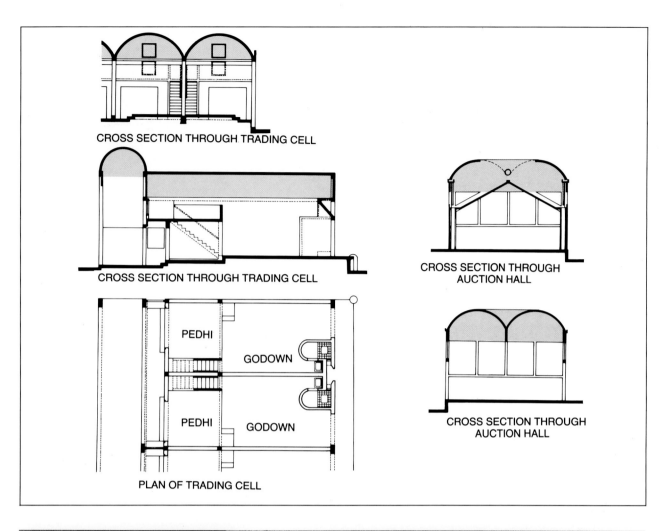

CROSS SECTION THROUGH TRADING CELL

CROSS SECTION THROUGH TRADING CELL

CROSS SECTION THROUGH
AUCTION HALL

CROSS SECTION THROUGH
AUCTION HALL

PEDHI

GODOWN

PEDHI

GODOWN

PLAN OF TRADING CELL

## Indian Institute of Management, Bangalore

Architect: Balkrishna Doshi – Stein Doshi and Bhalla;
K. Varkey, R. S. Kadakia,
H. V. Nagendra, B. J. Poonater
(associate architects)

Client: Indian Institute of Management

Consultants: Mahendra Raj – Engineering Consultants India (structure)

Contractors: Gina Engineering and South India Corporation Private Limited (educational block); Balagi Engineers and Construction Works (students' hostels)

Year of Completion: 1983 (Phase I)

Area: 13,000 m$^2$

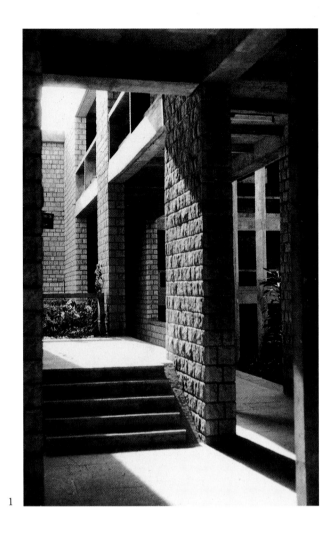

1

An urbanistic composition of courtyards, rich and varied in their architectural texture, is the theme of this labyrinthine academic complex. The buildings are rendered in an evocative mix of heavy building stone and delicate concrete, pregnant with allusions to traditional built form yet firmly grounded in the language of Modern architecture. A semi-formal landscape threads through the complex in the manner of a Mughal garden.

The programme for this institute includes a library (still under construction), extensive lecture and seminar spaces, faculty offices, cafeteria, lounges, and a separate compound of hostels and dining facilities for the students. The extensive colony of staff housing that adjoins the campus was a seprate commission designed by the office of Achyut Kanvinde.

The academic complex, including faculty offices and administration, is clustered along a major circulation spine running north-south. Four wings of offices, with open garden courts between, extend to the west at right angles to the spine; teaching spaces forming more complex arms and nodes, follow a loose checkerboard pattern around lesser courts to the east. The hostel blocks form a calico grid of quadrangles skewed at 45 degrees to the main campus.

The grey monotony of the exterior is relieved within the complex by the soft and varied play of light through the multivalent structure. This layered transparency is particularly rich along the circulation spine. There is an underlying, geometric order to the whole in spite of these many surprises and apparent eccentricities.

3

4

5

*Previous page*
1. Link to a garden court
2. Series of interlocking courts

3. Classroom wing under construction
4. Dormitory court
5. Academic wing, view from garden court
6. Trellised link between dormitories and teaching block

*Overleaf*
7. Outdoor court adjoining classrooms
8. Stair and corridor detail, dormitory
9. Layering of circulation spine and ancillary spaces

6

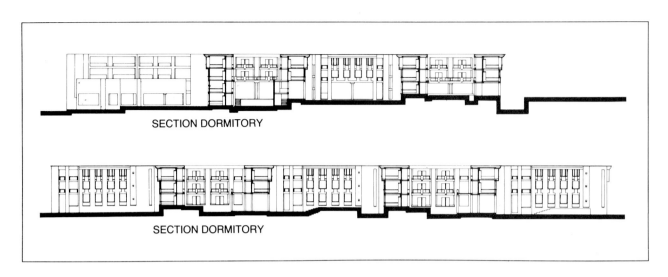

SECTION DORMITORY

SECTION DORMITORY

7

8

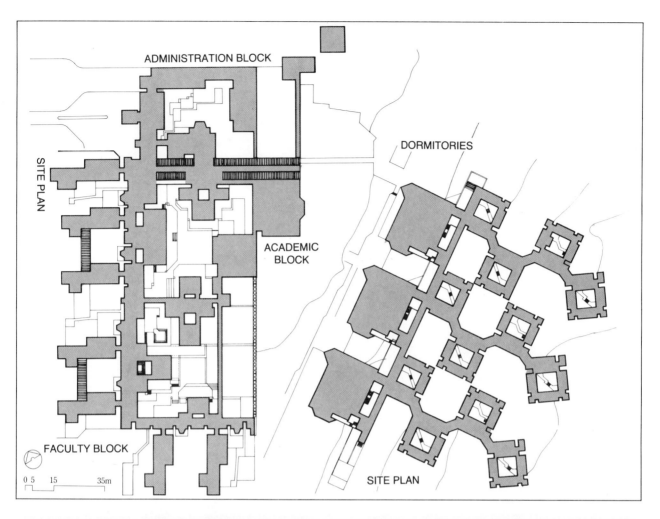

ADMINISTRATION BLOCK

SITE PLAN

DORMITORIES

ACADEMIC
BLOCK

FACULTY BLOCK

0 5   15        35m

SITE PLAN

CLASS ROOM-8

Administrative Office Complex,
Madhya Pradesh Electricity Board,
Jabalpur

Architect: Balkrishna Doshi – Stein
Doshi and Bhalla;
S. L. Bhavsar (project architect)

Client: Madhya Pradesh Electricity
Board

Consultants: Stein Doshi and Bhalla (services)

Contractor: Tarapore and Company

Year of Completion: 1987 (Phase I)

Area: 43,000 m²

Perched on a ridge above the city, this rambling palisade of government offices cannot help but remind one of the palace fortresses from which India's former rajas ruled the land. This image is almost explicit in the stout convoluted massing of the complex, but, characteristic of this architect, the gesture is elusive. The geometry and the language of the architecture are thoroughly contemporary. The building houses the bureaucracy of a major state utility, the key white-collar employer in this central Indian city. It is a large and lavish project by any standards; evidence of the political dimension of the architecture as a symbol of development. The building's public role is fulfilled with cultural and recreational facilities, such as an auditorium and the landscaped park and lake on the slopes below the complex.

The building contains 43,500 square metres of floor space organized in manageable increments as a network of interlocking octagons. The geometry will allow for orderly expansion in the future, while it has also given the architect planning flexibility to tailor the low-rise complex to the rugged, boulder-strewn site. The departmental hierarchy of a complicated bureaucracy has in reality been neatly managed by the incremental breakdown of the building. In general office areas, each octagon is crowned with a large skylight. A central void carries daylight down to open-plan work areas on several levels. Private offices and conference rooms are grouped on the periphery with windows to the exterior. Care is also taken to provide periodic exterior views from the central work areas. Exquisite wood fenestration is recessed into the undulating masonry enclosure for protection from the direct sun. The exterior is finished in a cement plaster with an aggregate of purple-brown stone chips, and highlighted with strips of polished granite. The moody play of shade and shadow on this dark exterior is punctuated by expressed circulation nodes in fair-faced concrete. Elevators, entrance halls and stairs are concentrated at these points in an exciting play of light and space that owes much to the architecture of Louis Kahn.

4

2

3

5

6

7

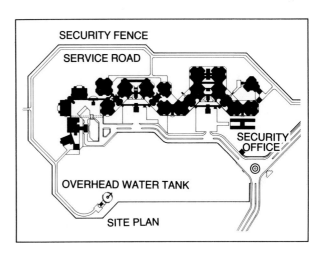

SECURITY FENCE

SERVICE ROAD

SECURITY OFFICE

OVERHEAD WATER TANK

SITE PLAN

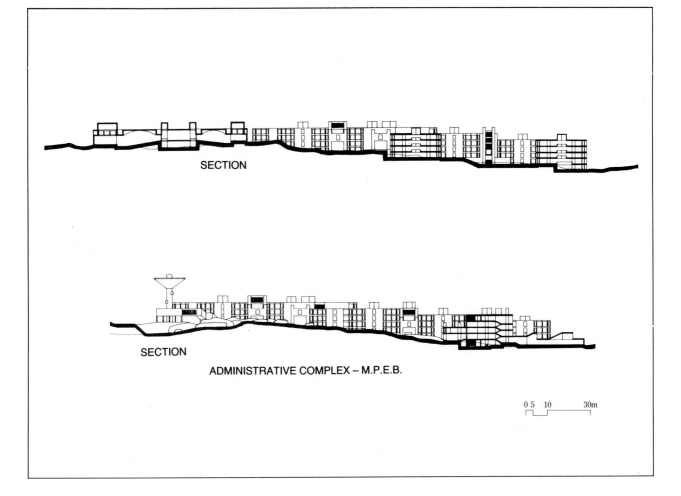

SECTION

SECTION

ADMINISTRATIVE COMPLEX – M.P.E.B.

0 5 10      30m

# 3. ALTERNATIVES FOR A DEVELOPING INDIA

*". . . In the context of the Third World, the architect must have the courage to face very disturbing issues. For what is your moral right to decide for a thousand, for a hundred thousand, for two millon people? But then what is the moral advantage in not acting, in merely watching passively the slow degradation of life around you . . . ?" Charles Correa[1]*

Anyone who builds in India today must confront the physical and economic realities of under-development. Much of the most interesting contemporary Indian architecture embodies the frugality, and even the primitiveness of the circumstances in which it is built as the basis for an expression of identity. This is, however, a passive response to the issues. Such buildings reflect reality — both the problems and the potential of a developing society — but rarely do they contribute to the process of change.

The socialist undertones of the Modernist ethic have compelled many architects to consider how design and planning might be more active agents of change. However, only a few in India manage to put such ideas into practice for the issues are so large, that potential activists are defeated by the apparent futility of even trying to make an impact. The architect's challenge is as much to find a relevant avenue by which to apply his skills as it is to innovate effective solutions. It is not surprising, therefore, that the handful of architects who regard themselves as committed activists see their work as a conscientious alternative to the conventional design processes and standard solutions of a profession oriented intrinsically to serve the advantaged classes of Indian society. But this attempt to engage in the process of development does not compromise the possibility of designing and building a full-blooded architecture. It simply recognizes a different set of parameters that can nevertheless pose a stimulating challenge to the practising architect. An innovative professionalism characterizes the design work behind some of India's more ambitious development initiatives in crucial areas such as urban housing.

In most of the developing nations, including India, to design for the poor appears to imply a search for appropriate Third World solutions to the desperate need for housing and basic amenities in fast-growing human settlements. The prevalence of such thinking is emphasized by the importance many professionals and political leaders engaged in development issues place on the use of the term 'Third World' in lieu of concepts such as 'underdeveloped' or 'developing'. This was a label originally coined by Jawaharlal Nehru and the other founders of the Non-Aligned Movement, to describe a third option — the open-ended alternative not to conform — that the emerging post-colonial nations wished to protect in defiance of the development options presented by the two Super Powers.[2] Although the politically shrewd idea of the Third World option continues to embody a certain optimism and flexibility in contemporary affairs, the term has become hackneyed. Many of the problems faced by developing societies are not necessarily unique, but it can be convenient to assign these a special status and avoid the hard-nosed criteria of the real world.

A Third World standard for design is, at best, an innovative response to the challenges posed by limited funds and resources; a creative rethinking of tools, methods and materials towards novel and effective solutions to demoralizing. problems. But to resort to an alternative standard, defined not so much by alternate, more relevant criteria, but by the conspicuous rejection of accepted norms can be a form of escapism that risks encouraging amateurism and mediocrity as acceptable qualities for an architecture oriented to the disadvantaged masses.

In a limited way Third World sensibilities can provide useful insights to the interpretation of crises that the development activist must address. The nature of

*Opposite page*
Library tower (see p.128)

possible solutions can be revealed in a problem that is sympathetically defined. But there is the possibility of going too far with such an alternative interpretation, of idealizing the forms and principles observed in lieu of simply assessing them with an unprejudiced eye. If the product of that analysis — a Third World architecture — becomes merely an attempt to simulate by design the spontaneous 'architecture without architects' of the evolving Third World city, then the value of the architect's contribution to the development process remains questionable.

The cities of the developing world are undergoing change with speed and violence. However, the conventional notion of progress, which implies imbibing the Western-style standard of living, does not necessarily describe this cataclysmic transformation. The important questions are: What is the Third World city evolving towards, and what direction should its architects and planners be providing? Is this Third World consciousness permanent or merely a transitional alternative to the ideals of modernization promoted by the Socialist and Western blocks? Is there something fundamentally different about human society in the poorer countries of the present day that should continue to distinguish them as Third World in a more evenly developed, more equitable global community of the future? Is it the architect's prerogative to decide, for example, that poor rural migrants to the Indian cities are culturally incapable of enjoying a modern house?

On a cultural level there is no doubt that a great diversity does and should continue to exist in the ways that the different peoples and subcultures of India — let alone the world — perceive and interpret daily life. But there is a stage at which a global culture ultimately takes root, one that universally shares much of what is already taken for granted in the way of communications, transport, industrial technology and international trade amongst other things, in the societies of the Third World. Where then does the threshold between the unique and the universal lie, and to which aspect of this reality should the architect apply his skills in the cause of development?

These questions cannot be categorically answered. There is a fundamental ambiguity in much of the work examined here. On the one hand political and philosophical idealism tends to distance and obscure the complexity of the issues. On the other hand stand the cynics who are convinced that all efforts are futile in view of the colossal problems at hand. An almost Machiavellian will to combat such fatalism with creative new possibilities complements the pragmatism evident in some of the more inspiring examples of 'alternative' architectural design in India.

## ACTIVISTS AND CONSULTANTS

Indian architects are working at various levels of the national development effort. The range of problems they address is dramatic and often they entail responsibilities other than the physical planning of the built environment. Economics and the political and sociological dimensions of the issues involved give the impetus for much that is most interesting in this work but, not surprisingly, they are also the key to some important failings.

At one extreme, a desire for political solidarity and immediacy to the issues encourages some activists to step out of their middle-class mould into the life of the poor themselves. Hands-on architects of this missionary ilk are usually limited in the scope of their efforts to the immediate communities with which they work. In some instances, however, efforts to transfer appropriate new skills and technology to a small client group can have a wider impact through example to other communities.

At the other end of the spectrum, independent architectural consultants have been successful collaborators with government in promoting effective alternatives to the stale or outmoded formulas for housing and urban development commonly applied by government planning departments. Although this is a limited and external form of design intervention, its potential influence can be enormous. The planning of New Bombay is a good illustration of this point.

The current strategy for the growth and development of the greater metropolitan region of Bombay was originally conceived and advocated by an independent lobby of concerned architects. It has since been adopted by government and gradually implemented. It will be instructive to describe the scheme briefly as it demonstrates some of the more effective principles by which planners and architects have structured their assault on development issues in India.

The idea for New Bombay was first proposed in 1964 by the architect Charles Correa in collaboration with Pravina Mehta and Shirish Patel. Their suggestions were forward-looking but realistic: to co-ordinate and enhance government initiatives involving new highways, bridges and industrial zoning; to expand and transform a critically congested linear city into a ring-like, polycentred city on the water. This was to be accomplished by providing an infrastructure and incentives that would encourage new nodes of growth on the undeveloped shores opposite the long narrow peninsula on which the original port city of Bombay was built (Fig. 3.1).[3]

The plan for New Bombay did not entail a revolutionary transformation of the existing urban organism of Bombay. It was a proposal for a planned redirection of future growth using the economic, demographic and political forces already in play. A more evenly distributed urban network would offer healthy new options for economic competition and new space to house the urban poor in reasonable proximity to the jobs that would be created. The strategy for implementation was pragmatic. Although a solution to the housing crises of the less privileged inhabitants of Bombay was a primary objective, the designers were shrewd enough to acknowledge that jobs were the first priority of the urban poor; economics was the concern of government. These facts were exploited to indirectly support the social and environmental benefits of the scheme.

This micro-economic approach to urban and regional planning is being adapted, on a smaller scale, to the design and implementation of specific housing schemes.

## HUMAN SETTLEMENTS PROGRAMMES

Housing, within the broader issue of human settlements, is the aspect of India's formal development effort with which the architectural profession is most significantly involved. However, it is not as a conventional designer of houses that the architect has much to contribute. The issue is too large and resources too limited for relevant and cost-effective efforts to be made at that intimate level. The architect's ability to preconceive the complex set of relationships between people, their physical environment, and the influential parameters of economics, culture and tradition, is of greater consequence. Architects' efforts to structure the dwelling environment at the community level in some current Indian housing initiatives are interesting exercises in refining the mechanistic housing strategies of most formal development agencies. Again, the more successful examples of architectural intervention in this field reflect the designer's willingness to acknowledge and work with the inevitable constraints of the problem. These include the patterns and tendencies that spontaneously emerge in any growing settlement. This willingness to 'play the game' with skill and innovation, extends to an acceptance of the frugal logic that the Indian government and most international development agencies have adopted in their housing programmes of recent years. Development policies today tend to recognize the spontaneous growth process in human settlements as a force far superior, and in many regards more efficient and more accurate than the pre-designed and built form of housing that the formal sector has tried to provide in the past.

Since the early seventies Indian authorities have endorsed a human settlements planning concept that promotes user initiative in building housing for the poor. In such 'sites-and-services' projects the layout and preparation of building plots with essential services — roads, water supply, storm and waste water drainage, and sometimes, a small structure containing a toilet — is the only responsibility undertaken by the formal sector, while the design and construction of actual dwellings is left to the owners of each plot (Fig. 3.2). Economy is the primary objective of this strategy; minimum resources are allocated to each individual such that a maximum number of people — of a set economic target group — can be reached with at least the rudiments of housing within the fixed funding for a given development. From a design standpoint, a distinct advantage of this approach is its inherent flexibility that allows individuals to meet their own specific needs to a degree of variation and detail that has been impossible to provide in conventionally planned public housing developments.

The sites-and-services strategy is essentially cost-effective, not a no-cost answer to the need for better housing and communal amenities, and most efforts in this area have not reached the poorest segments of society. In practice, projects are targeted at narrowly defined lower-income groups who have some

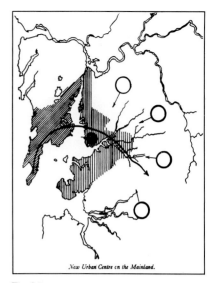

Fig. 3.1
Plan of New Bombay.

Fig. 3.2
View of a Sites-and-Services Project.

91

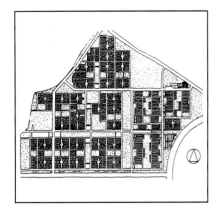

Fig. 3.3
Plan of a Sites-and-Services Project.

resources to invest in their housing. However, many of the homeless cannot afford to spend their marginal incomes on shelter. Economic opportunity and proximity to the place of work are greater priorities than the desire for a permanent dwelling.

A problem stemming from the economic priorities of both the planners and users of many sites-and-services projects is the tendency to compromise or simply ignore the socio-cultural dimensions of domestic and communal life. For the sake of economy in planning and managing a development, different income groups are often ghettoized, plot designs and street layouts are relentlessly standardized, and only marginal attention is devoted to the planning of public spaces (Fig. 3.3). The argument that more attractive design must necessarily be sacrificed as an expensive luxury is accepted, unfortunately, by most architects who see no place for their skills in such low-cost planning efforts. With this regrettable impasse between architects and government engineers, even the questionable cost-effectiveness of some of the more mechanistic planning practices applied in such schemes has gone unchallenged. Gradually, experience is showing that insufficiently and insensitively designed sites-and-services projects can degenerate into a quality of environment only superior to most squatter settlements by virtue of their functional services.

These practical failings of the sites-and-services concept do not, however, undermine the fundamental pragmatism and potential it retains as a basis for effective design intervention in the development process. As long as poverty is the primary reality, the need for economic solutions will be overriding. But to counteract the shortcomings of a merely mechanical equation between the financial resources of an individual and the maximum material amenities he can be provided with, there is a call for a much more dynamic manipulation of the problem at a micro-economic level. What is essential is to abandon the idea of a single target group, and to consider, alternatively, a complete economic cross-section of society as a developing community. In this sense the designing of housing ceases to be viewed as a finite project. As with large-scale urban designs, housing is better conceived as a co-ordinated development scenario that encourages the enrichment and diversification of the end product by setting up a creative interaction between a wide cross-section of users and beneficiaries. This strategy has been successfully employed in recent urban projects in Madras and Kanpur, implemented by their respective municipal authorities with financial and technical assistance from the World Bank.

In a recent proposal for a large public housing scheme in the central Indian city of Indore, a team of architects and engineers from the Vastu-Shilpa Foundation in Ahmedabad have developed this broad-based alternative application of the sites-and-services strategy to a considerable degree of refinement. The active basis for the proposal is socio-economic; a controlled manipulation of the marked and sometimes contentious communalism inherent in Indian urban culture. Rather than idealizing a non-existent social homogeneity, the scheme acknowledges that each income group with its various religious and ethnic subdivisions, has its own requirements and capacities, but often another group will provide a service or a market to meet those demands. Combined in a co-ordinated community development scenario, the sites-and-services incentives conventionally reserved for low-income target groups are also tailored to the housing and commercial requirements of affluent middle-class merchants and professionals. Such diversification creates a healthy tax base as well as autonomous commercial activity within the settlement, both of which can serve to cross-subsidize the cost of land and services for the homeless poor who would otherwise be unable to hold on to even the most rudimentary government furnished plot.

To make this principle of cross-subsidization really work the architects have maintained an explicit hierarchy between the different economic categories of plot recipients in the scheme. For instance, the fundamentally separate space and access requirements of automobile-driving externally oriented upper-income residents are clearly differentiated from the pedestrian-based lifestyle and spatial order of the lower-income neighbourhoods that form the heart of the scheme. Despite these demarcations the whole scheme is sensitively integrated. A distinctive network of public spaces within the 7,000-plot development reflects the designers' attempt to improve on the inefficient redundancy of the standard cartesian layout of plots and services used in conventional sites-and-services developments. In the same exercise, short streets, *chowks* (small public open spaces) and *mohallas* (narrow pedestrian alleys) are implied in the layout; there is a sympathetic sequence from the public realm to more private protected space at the level of each plot. As both rich and poor residents are responsible for all construction, the architects' task has been to anticipate the outcome of a spontaneous process by designing the unbuilt spaces and relationships that will stimulate the desired growth.

The social and economic virtues of diversity in the planning of human settlements have been recognized in various Indian housing efforts of recent years. However, the subtle but important differences between developments such as the Indore township and the Artistes' Village, a housing scheme within the larger planning framework of New Bombay, show some significant divergences in the social ideals propounded.

The Artistes' Village is an experimental housing sector completed in 1986; a realized increment of the broad scenario for New Bombay that the architect, Charles Correa, formulated some twenty years earlier. Though it has only 700 plots as compared to the 7,000-plot Indore scheme, the intentions of the two developments are similar — to house a variety of income groups in a single integrated neighbourhood. Village-like in imagery and in its apparently loose and random order, the overall development is rendered in a curious neo-vernacular that might have been conceived by a village *mistri* (traditional builder) were it not so religiously and rigidly cloned from one standard unit type to the next. No dwelling units actually touch one another, even though plots are small and tightly clustered to create an integrated network of semi-private and public spaces.

An obvious difference between this development and most recent government sponsored housing efforts is that the dwelling units are pre-built — at least in rudimentary form — and, as such, the architectural character of the settlement has been narrowly prescribed. The implications of the imagery employed are interesting in their own right and we shall return to that point in a moment. Of greater importance, however, is the scheme's underlying principle of *equity* that this folksy and homogeneous expression serves to advertise. Despite the social disparities between the various income groups incorporated in the development, the architecture and the egalitarian principles by which plots are clustered and distributed do their best to disguise these differences. The basic units do vary in size and type but only according to a prescribed series of incremental additions and combinations that respects the common code of elements, proportions and scale. Each household is able to expand within this controlled pattern of growth to the extent of its financial means and space requirements. The collective standard of the housing furnishes an image of domestic bliss that exceeds the average lot of the poorer residents. But the converse is also true, which raises doubts about the viability of such a concept as a spontaneous development scenario. In the mixed-income scheme proposed for Indore, on the other hand, it is by catering opportunistically to the wealthier home-builder and his natural desire to invest more money in more exclusive real estate that an effective trade-off in resources and capital is realized. Such entrepreneurial pragmatism is likely to give a more dependable impetus to the growth of a community, than the altruistic ideal that those more fortunate will voluntarily opt for a more collective, equitable lifestyle.

Correa has portrayed his housing experiment in New Bombay as a fragment of the 'new landscape' he foresees for the Third World city of the future.[4] The rustic, scenographic character of his architecture is thus a surprising indication of the manner of urban experience that it might entail. One cannot help seeing in these petite cottages with their colourful shutters and exaggerated gables, the chimera of a movie-village, like the idyllic pastiches that dot the back-lots of Bombay's film studios. The fantasy promised by that generic caricature of tropical vernacular is in many regards a parallel to the garden city ideal promoted in the nineteenth century as an antidote to the coal-blackened squalor of industrial England. Effectively, the Artistes' Village is a classic suburban alternative to the intensity of city life; a tract of tiny single-family bungalows linked by a (projected) mass transit system to the heart of India's most important metropolis. A collective, pre-industrial order remains the untenable ideal of the development.

## ARCHITECTURE WITHOUT ARCHITECTS

The longing for a simple village way of life — with its implications of greater self-sufficiency, environmental harmony, and social co-operation — has characterized most of the utopian thinking that has emerged in the wake of the industrial conquest of the world over the last two centuries. William Morris, Ebenezer Howard, John Ruskin and Jean-Jacques Rousseau were some of the more obvious Western predecessors in this philosophical tradition. It is no surprise that the admiring student of European liberal thought, Mohandas Gandhi, and the rustic ideal he cherished as the desired path for India's development have served as the fulcrum for most alternative ideology and social activism in modern India.

Through the last two decades, a new crop of nostalgic iconoclasts have captured a following among architects and social planners. In his book *Small is Beautiful: a study of economics as if people mattered*, E. F. Schumacher provided a blueprint for a co-operative, proto-industrial approach to life and work that guided many counter-cultural experiments through the 1960s and 1970s. Bernard Rudofsky's sweeping celebration of vernacular craftsmanship in *Architecture Without Architects* and subsequent books, has been another influential polemic in an era that has become increasingly sceptical of the idea of progress. Such sympathetic external influences have reinforced the stamp of Gandhi on the work and attitude of various Indian activists.

Respectfully deified as the spiritual father of the modern Indian nation but generally ignored by economic planners, Gandhi was the underdog in the unbridled push toward industrialization and urbanism following India's independence. Through time and the problematic experiences of modernization, Gandhi's ideals have held their ground, with no shortage of defenders, as an almost sacred alternative to formal development policies. However, this veneration has often tended to blur good judgement in the translation of those convictions into social action. A basic premise of Gandhianism is that Indian culture is still rooted in the village, and that society should continue to develop within the self-nurturing security of that rural order. But one may argue that the reality is different. A large portion of society, although still in the minority, has long ago graduated to an urban frame of mind, and thrived. The forced and unconvincing gesture of solidarity with the village exhibited in proposals for an alternative lifestyle, such as the Artistes' Village, provokes one to question whether this desire to retreat from the city is truly the will of the collective or merely the sentimental nostalgia of the urbanized elite.

A necessary counterpart to Gandhi's philosophy of development is a commitment to live by it; the activist should provide leadership through personal example. This demand appeals to a variety of architects who have opted to sacrifice conventional architectural practice and engage themselves fully in what might be called 'grassroots initiatives'. Among them are proponents of Schumacher's intermediate technocracy whose hands-on experiments with an ecological approach to design frequently amount to a committed personal pursuit of an alternative lifestyle. Others, such as the British-Indian architect Laurie Baker and his admirers, remain more focused in their professional calling but place much emphasis on both the practical and altruistic aspects of participating in the physical process of building. Yet another category — those involved in social action at the community level — respond most directly to the Gandhian compulsion to help the poor on a personal and interactive basis.

Grassroots community work is best illustrated in the projects and programmes of small non-governmental development organizations. Groups such as Unnayan in Calcutta, Development Alternatives in Delhi, and the Ahmedabad Study Action Group have established themselves in most of the larger Indian cities. As multi-disciplinary action lobbies comprising a variety of professionals — architects, planners, economists and community workers — such organizations work to develop an interface between people in need and the institutions and infrastructure that can help them. The role the architect plays in this manner of team work is much broader than that of the conventional professional. It may entail diverse organizational and decision-making responsibilities but little physical design. Housing is a component of this work but usually a subset of comprehensive social programmes involving education, health, nutrition, vocational development, and so on.

Several of the important community action groups in India have developed out of the independent initiatives of their architectural members to apply their professional skills to the needs of the poor. Therefore, the low profile of architectural design in their work is intriguing. The shortage of resources and capital in many of the working situations they deal with can only partially explain this, as such constraints are common to all low-cost design efforts. The conflicts and biases generated by the grassroots methods of these activists offer a more explicit explanation for this apparently self-imposed constraint on creative architectural thinking.

The economic viability of community action lobbies is precarious. To work directly for poor client groups, activists must first identify problems and create their own commissions, obtaining sanctions and funding from government and formal development agencies. This presents an ethical dilemma for the architect, as his professional relationships with these various clients become confused. The necessity of fabricating design commissions, if not the problems themselves, also calls into doubt the appropriateness of his services at this intimate level of commitment. Social and economic initiatives are inevitably easier to justify in the hierarchy of development concerns.

These professional scruples are compounded by the politics of community action. The ideal of democratic, people-oriented development runs contrary to the concept of the architect as an elite form-giver. The reaction is to transfer responsibility for architectural design to the users themselves. The architect assumes a background role as a skilled organizer who can translate their ideas into action. User-initiative has been increasingly exploited in the planned development of human settlements in India, but an important difference between the sites-and-services experiments discussed earlier and such independent grass-roots programmes lies in the direct involvement of the lay public in the formal design process. The architect's own creative prerogative is curtailed, a voluntary censorship that appears to imply a loss of faith in the profession's capacity to address the real issues. Curiously, action becomes relevant for these architects when they discard the skills they are most qualified to apply.

## APPROPRIATE TECHNOLOGIES

The introspective tendency of the socially conscious professional is mirrored in the efforts of some architects to promote the concept of an appropriate technology as the answer to India's development needs. Ostensibly this is a pragmatic plea to extend limited resources in view of the extreme demands placed on the environment by the forces of population and industrial progress. But the implications of the solutions offered are far greater than simply being a question of alternative technique. The compulsion of its practitioners is to personally demonstrate not only the building methods, but the whole alternative lifestyle that would give meaning to the voluntary suspension of technological progress they propose. This compulsion is a measure of the almost religious nature of that ideal.

The movement for an appropriate technology gathered most of its impetus in the rich industrialized nations of the West when, in 1973 the Organization of Petroleum Exporting Countries created an artificial shortage of oil in the world market. This so-called energy crisis brought into sharp focus the disturbing reality of those nations that were acutely dependent on limited resources subject to political manipulation. The perennial ideal of a simpler, self-supporting mode of life was subsequently accorded serious attention. In countries such as the United States, official research programmes to develop alternative autonomous sources of energy were complemented by a massive campaign to make the public conscious of the need to conserve. A reassessment of the patterns of energy consumption and the careless waste of affluent societies was advocated as a key to averting a real crisis. This initiative reinforced an already well-entrenched concern for the fragility of the natural environment in a machine dominated world. A consequence of the reduced consumption of petroleum-based energy would be a reduction of waste and pollutants. The two concerns came together, creatively, in the surge of innovative proposals for the passive, low-impact production, use and re-use of energy that came to be labelled as 'appropriate technology'.

In the sphere of architecture the ramifications of this conservation consciousness were a broad range of experiments with alternative building materials, structures, and passive systems for the climatic control of the built environment. The effort to diminish dependence on industrial production encouraged the investigation of organic materials and manual methods of construction. A renewed interest in vernacular building technology and its aesthetics was a natural corollary of this research.

Fig. 3.4
A Typical Bio-Gas Plant Installation.

The most significant flaw in the appropriate technologists' argument has been the backward leap in standards of living that their anti-industrial, anti-urban alternatives entail. The advanced countries have become conscious of ecological issues in recent years, and efforts to avert the threat posed to the environment by progress have been all the more forward-looking. Industry has led the way with new technology of a much higher sophistication and efficiency, neutralizing many ecological concerns while advancing the standards of comfort and leisure. The alternative movement has remained an idealistic counter-culture to the affluent society and its values. Meanwhile, alternative technologists have shifted their focus to the more accommodating context of the developing countries. From the pre-industrial perspective of the Third World village, the philosophy of optimizing the use of local resources and labour promises tangible results, such as improved agricultural output, cottage industry and innovative low-cost housing, all of which constitute a plausible, intermediate alternative to the uncertain rewards of full-fledged industrialization.

In India, the enthusiasm for appropriate technology is exhibited in the programmes of many Gandhian organizations. Government has also attempted to promote the use of technologies, such as methane gas plants to reduce village-level dependence on conventional energy resources (Fig. 3.4). The efforts of architects in this direction have been more isolated, often in the form of model ecological homesteads and communities. In form and philosophy, this architecture is still directly linked to Western counter culture; it has not seen widespread application to building problems and human settlement issues in the country as a whole.

A forum for some of the most interesting experimentation with appropriate technology in India is the international settlement of Auroville. About five hundred people, many of them Europeans, comprise the permanent population of this cosmopolitan community on the south-east coast of India. As in most utopian experiments, the impetus for this exercise in communal and environmental harmony is spiritual. The settlement is being conceived as a vision of a united global society, its pioneering settlers committed to the teachings of the late mystic, Sri Aurobindo.

Auroville is a loose array of homesteads scattered over a development area of over twenty square kilometers. Small-scale, labour-intensive construction is a continuous activity along with cultivation, reforestation and various small-scale specialized industries. The handful of architects and engineers who have chosen to live in this community have built many innovative structures with minimum resources. A wide range of construction systems and materials have been experimented with in their buildings. For the most part they have explored the traditional uses of materials, such as bamboo, casuarina thatch, mud and stone and upgraded them where appropriate. Ordinary mud brick construction, for example, is susceptible to the torrential monsoons of south-east India. A more durable, monolithic form of mud construction known as 'rammed-earth', has been exploited in many Auroville structures in lieu of conventional masonry. Industrial materials are sparingly used, usually as lightweight, material-conserving technologies, such as ferro-cement, that can be manipulated by hand.

The buildings of Auroville serve the mundane functional requirements of the community, but their purpose, like the settlement itself, is to a much greater extent symbolic. The conscious act of building a low-cost, ecologically appropriate architecture is a form of devotion to the ideal of a better world that underlies such holistic social experiments. Despite the creative intent of those architects who have built here, their innovations only amount to tinkering within the preconceived economic and technological order they advocate as the appropriate model for the development of the Third World. The sense of a world apart cultivated in Auroville and other idyllic homesteading experiments by Indian architects suggests an escape from the difficult challenge of analysing and resolving socio-economic issues within the mandate of conventional architectural practice. The ritual of self-improvement serves as a placebo for the original ideas and creative conceptual thinking that so few architects seem to be able to bring to the problems of the poor.

Laurie Baker is an expatriate architect who has made his career in India, committed, in the Gandhian spirit, to the service of society. Like most grassroots activists he has felt compelled to alter the conventional practise of his profession in order to realize his altruistic objectives. Discernible in his work, however, is a primary commitment to the making of a highly personal architecture of quality. Baker's buildings gain character from the visually distinctive techniques he has devised for reducing construction costs. In his design method he takes pains to involve the eventual users of his buildings in making important decisions. But neither technical criteria nor sociological intent appear to outweigh the architect's confidence in his professional expertise and the ultimate authority of his own spontaneous creativity.

"... Low cost is a relative term, there is a false notion that low cost is only for the poor ...." What Baker practises is 'cost reduction', a principle and a variety of techniques that he applies to the needs of poor clients as well as the rich.[5] Middle-class professionals are his largest client group, a respected element of society whose collaboration with Baker in reducing the cost of building serves as an example to other factions who tend to be more fixed in their status-minded ideals about *pucca* (durable) construction.

Fig. 3.5
Trivandrum Museum.

Baker's architecture is an imaginative exploitation of exposed brick masonry. The cost-saving elimination of plaster unveils the graphic potential of brick and mortar. Rich textures are generated in varied bonding patterns and pointing, and in the ubiquitous use of the *jali*, a lattice of brick that diffuses light and admits the breeze. This sensitivity for the building craft suggests a bias towards the 'Arts and Crafts' ethic that prevailed in his British training of the 1930s. A benign anomaly in modern day India, his architecture has a strong affinity with the hybrid style of some of the more interesting British Indian buildings of the late Victorian and Edwardian eras (Fig. 3.5). In form, the buildings are evocative of a child's fantasy of gingerbread houses, with their corbelled arches, niches, built-in window seats and slit openings — the whole covered, in most instances, by a large wooden roof with many peaks and valleys. This expression is largely derived from the traditional architecture of India's southern-most state of Kerala where Baker lives and works (Fig. 3.6). A rationale common to wooden buildings throughout the coastal regions of South and South East Asia is exhibited in the overbearing size and drama of the roof with its large overhangs that keep heavy monsoon rains away from the interior spaces. Walls, on the other hand, are reduced to mere structure and screens to allow breezes to pass through the building.

Fig. 3.6
Padmanabhapuram Palace.

The message in Baker's work that appears to have earned the admiration of many Indian architects is that social commitment and creativity as an architect do not necessarily negate each other. But neither Baker, nor others, have managed to address the full scope of the issues. The grassroots tactic is overly empirical; activists manage to reach only a limited number of people from their alternative camp. Their work confirms that the architect who takes too righteous a position is prone to produce a naive and shallow architecture as the built manifestation of that belief. The more effective architects are those who acknowledge this ideological impasse through their pragmatic and conciliatory approach to the problem. In their work there is a consciousness that change must be introduced incrementally through the system itself. This attitude prevails over the more idealistic view that society, a community, or even an individual client will easily and willingly transform its lifestyle and — more importantly — its aspirations to accept the alternatives the architect may offer.

The Gandhian belief in the permanence of rural values continues to dominate the social concerns of Indian architects. In the jungles of Kerala and Maharashtra, or in the Aurovillians' attempt to create a world apart, these values may continue to hold for some time. In the urban context the probity of a timeless vernacular should be subjected to more scrutiny. A paternalistic sentimentality for the rustic ideal in the planning of new settlements could have the effect of trapping the urban poor in their underdeveloped past more surely than providing a familiar footing from which to move forward. The emerging reality of India's urban poor is only beginning to be examined for what it is. The question remains whether the lessons of the village are to be idealized or transitionally utilized towards a different future.

**NOTES:**

1. Charles Correa, *The New Landscape*, The Book Society of India, Bombay, 1985. p. 132.
2. Ibid., p. 6.
3. New Bombay: Draft Development Plan, City and Industrial Development Corporation of Maharashtra Limited, Bombay, 1973. pp. 7-11.
4. Correa. op.cit., pp. 54-64.
5. P.G. Varughese, 'A Questing Conscience', *Architecture + Design*, July-Aug 1985. pp. 12-27.

Aranya Township, Indore

Architect: Balkrishna Doshi –
Vastu-Shilpa Foundation,
Ahmedabad

Client: Indore Development
Authority

Consultant: Environmental Engineering Consultants
(infrastructure)
Under construction, 1988

Contractor: Departmental

Area: 7000 plot township on 86 hectare site

The Aranya housing project is a large township comprising about 7,000 plots for a projected population of approximately 65,000. Sited on the fringe of Indore, the project is intended to relieve an acute demand for housing in the city centre. The project is formulated on the formal sites-and-services strategy for large-scale housing initiatives. Prepared plots, services and communal infrastructure are provided by the Indore Development Authority; the construction of the actual dwellings is left to the users. The scheme has been designed for a majority of low-income residents; 65 per cent of the plots are reserved for the so-called economically weaker sections of society who earn less than Rs. 350 per month (approximately $ 30 per month). Separate plots for higher-income residents are integrated into the scheme. These are to be sold at a profit to cross-subsidize the costs of the lower income plots. Municipal sites-and-services design standards for plot sizes, service cores and infrastructure have been rigorously adhered to for the various low income plots. The designers have been innovative, however, in their efforts to optimize the economics of services and the sociological interplay of dense urban neighbourhoods. The scheme is characterized by a sophisticated, highly unconventional configuration of plots and public spaces.

To avoid segregating each income group while maintaining the marketability of higher income plots, the housing is organized in concentric rings. The periphery of each sector is ringed with large road-accessed plots; lower income blocks are contained within along with public facilities, such as kindergartens, schools, dispensaries and post offices. Large open areas are avoided. Public space is evenly distributed in small parcels. Short pedestrian cul-de-sacs are the smallest unit of communal space. These are actually service slots created by eliminating one or two plots from the regular back-to-back configuration of plots in a block. Such slots give access and an efficient single connection point for water and sewage to as many as six units at a time. This innovation requires that only every second street in a sector carry service mains thus effecting a reduction in projected infrastructural costs of about 30 per cent. Larger squares serve as nodes to interconnect the network of streets. A hierarchy of income generating activities from small vendors and cottage industries to a central market complex is built up through the network of public spaces.

The basic infrastructure of the Aranya township has been implemented to-date. It will be a few years before the residents occupy all the plots and the built form anticipated by the designers begins to emerge.

1. Part of a typical block, with service cores; to be built up by users.
2. Demonstration sector constructed as a design guide for future residents.
3. Architect's rendering of the anticipated street facade, as would be developed by future residents.

# Artiste's Village, Belapur, New Bombay

Architect: Charles Correa

Client: City and Industrial Development Corporation of Maharashtra Limited

Consultants: N/A

Contractor: N/A

Year of Completion: 1986

Area: 600 houses of varying sizes from 26 m$^2$ to 75 m$^2$

The Artiste's Village is a subdivision of a major urban development. Proposed mass transit will link it directly to Central Bombay. Thus, the village-like characteristics of the project constitute an explicit alternative to the most intensive urban living in India. The low-rise medium density of the scheme is not remarkable in itself, but it differs dramatically from neighbouring developments both in its imagery and in its carefully structured layout. It is the antithesis of the monotonous geometry, blocks and slabs that have characterized the standard functional approach to housing in India. The rustic, almost primitive appearance of the housing disguises the fact that most of the 500 plus units in the scheme are designed for middle and higher income consumer groups. This bohemian quality is envisaged as being particularly attractive to professional artists for whom 25 per cent of the units are reserved.

The objective of the scheme is to combine a range of different income groups and sub-communities in a coherent and equitable neighbourhood structure. All houses are free-standing and similarly detailed in a range of sizes and shapes. Plot areas are small (45 to 75 square metres), varied in proportion depending on unit type. The autonomy of each unit permits a modest degree of expansion and personalization. Houses are grouped in small clusters surrounding a courtyard of 8 x 8 metres. Three of these clusters form a larger module around a 12 x 12 metre space. Three such neighbourhood modules combine to define a still larger community *maidan*, which completes the hierarchy of public spaces. The housing is constructed with basic materials and low-tech building methods; clay tile roofs, smooth finish *neeru* (lime slurry) plaster interiors, sand finished cement plaster exteriors on brick bearing walls, *in situ* cement flooring.

A choice of prefabricated wooden doors and shutters is left to the home buyers. Given a greater opportunity to participate in the design process, users might have encouraged the architect to increase the prohibitively cramped proportions of the doll-house like individual units.

1. Model showing network of public and private spaces
2. Several units defining a semi-private court

*Overleaf*
3. Development under construction
4. Construction detail, lower income unit
5. Typical communal *chowk*

1

3

4

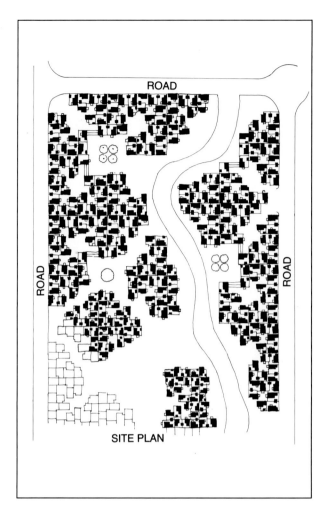

ROAD

ROAD

ROAD

ROAD

SITE PLAN

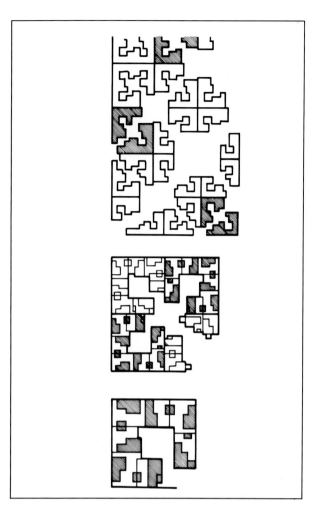

5

Integrated Urban Development
Project, Vasna, Ahmedabad

Architect: Kirtee Shah – Ahmedabad
Study Action Group

Client: Ahmedabad Municipal
Corporation

Contractor: Built under direct supervision of the
architect

Year of Completion: 1975

Area: 2248 units at 24 m² each on a 10 hectare site

Many migrants flock to Ahmedabad, the largest industrial centre in Gujarat, in search of jobs. A large percentage of these labourers and their families settle in squatter settlements on the low-lying banks of the Sabarmati river which passes through the centre of the city. During the 1973 monsoon floods more than 3,000 of these families lost their huts and found themselves on the sidewalks of the city. It was the Ahmedabad Study Action Group, a multidisciplinary team of development activists, who came to their aid with an ambitious disaster relief plan entailing not only new housing but programmes for their social and economic advancement. These programmes included neighbourhood organization, adult education and income supplementation schemes. The group's proposal was adopted by the Ahmedabad Municipal Corporation and implemented with additional financial support from OXFAM, the Housing and Urban Development Corporation and the Gujarat State Government. The new settlement was laid out on a 10 hectare site, 8 kilometres from the city centre. It consists of 2,248 low-cost dwelling units with additional infrastructure including community buildings.

An achievement of this project was the direct participation of the dwellers in the design of the housing. Individual unit plans were developed in two stages. First, members of the design team circulated large-scale models of proposed design units among the users. People's comments and reactions were noted with the help of social workers and used to improve the designs. The second stage involved the actual building of eight full-scale demonstration houses. Additional feedback from the anticipated users resulted in significant changes.

A typical two-room dwelling unit is built of exposed brick with asbestos cement roofs. It has a veranda at the front and a shared courtyard at the rear. Four units have access to this space and a common set of services, including an outdoor wash place. Intensive shared use of this court for kitchen and other domestic activities has been the cause of some social friction. In most cases, however, it has proven to be a successful answer to the limited space and resources.

One drawback of the project is its distance from the city centre, the place of work for most residents. As a result, some of the original occupants have sold their properties (at profit) and have moved back to squatter settlements downtown.

1. Informal classroom in semi-public open space
2. Row of typical units facing street
   *Overleaf*
3. Model of typical block with shared service courts
4. Series of shaded community courts
5. Site model

1

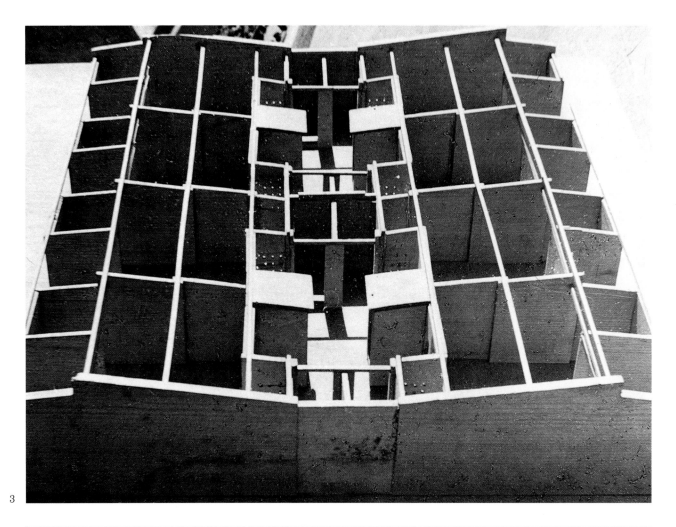

3

4

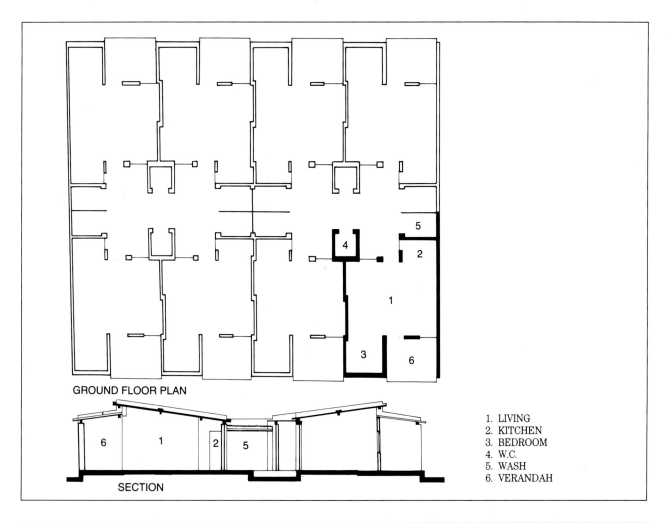

GROUND FLOOR PLAN

SECTION

1. LIVING
2. KITCHEN
3. BEDROOM
4. W.C.
5. WASH
6. VERANDAH

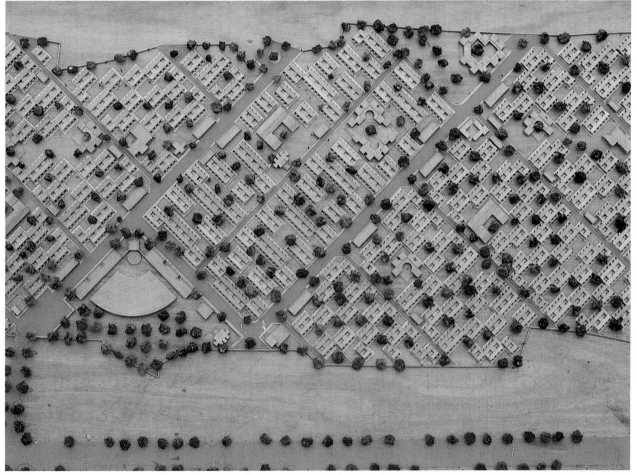

Aspiration Huts, Auroville

Architects: Piero Cicionesi and
Gloria Cicionesi

Client: Auroville community

Contractor: Built under direct supervision of the
architects

Year of Completion: 1971

Area: 2936 m$^2$ (18 square units at 58 m$^2$ each, 16
hexagonal units at 62 m$^2$ each)

Over the past two decades some adventurous experiments with alternative technologies for building and living in resource deficient conditions have taken place at the experimental international settlement of Auroville near Pondicherry on India's south-east coast. Imbued with a pioneering spirit many of the residents have participated in building the settlement from scratch. Their philosophical and logistical commitment to low-impact, low-energy building methods has inspired a variety of interesting 'do-it-yourself' structures. The handful of professional architects in the community have been responsible for broader planning issues and the design of common facilities.

The Aspiration Huts were among the first buildings to be erected at Auroville, the work of a husband and wife team of Italian architects newly arrived in India. In this pioneering project a precedent was established for many of the tendencies observed in the design and construction techniques of later Auroville structures. The huts were designed as temporary accommodation for the original residents of the settlement, a group housing scheme comprising 34 units and a community kitchen. The hut-like breakdown of the housing gives the impression of a tropical village,

though distinct in its form and order from the Tamil village that adjoins the site. A strong geometric rigour underlines this informality. The tidy clustering of volumes and hierarchical separation of service and served spaces testifies to the European modernist training of the architects, exercised here with the special challenge of a pre-industrial context. There are two unit types. Half of these are based on the square; the remainder on a hexagonal geometry, all paired in semi-detached clusters. Type one is composed of 2 square chambers linked by a corridor with built-in storage and bathroom. The hexagon-based units have three chambers fused together as a contiguous space. The storage and bathroom wing is contiguous with the adjoining unit. Roofs are the dominant feature of the architecture; wooden structures sheathed with casuarina thatch transpose the base geometry into three dimensions. These float above a low terraced and sculpted plinth of smooth faced concrete. Air flows freely through the structures and light is admitted through innovative — though slightly clumsy — triangular shutters that can be swung inwards or outwards against the slope of the roof.

1. Interior view, Aspiration huts.
2. Larger thatched dwelling structure
3. Cluster, Aspiration huts

*Overleaf*
4. Aspiration huts
5. Sleeping bay, Aspiration huts
6. Tree house, early experiment with bamboo and thatch
7. Early Auroville experiments with light weight wood construction.

1

3

2

4

5

6

7

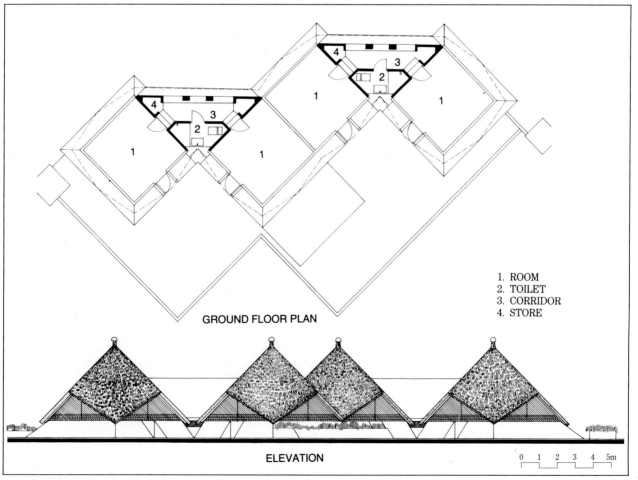

GROUND FLOOR PLAN

1. ROOM
2. TOILET
3. CORRIDOR
4. STORE

ELEVATION

0 1 2 3 4 5m

Sanskrit School, Auroville

Architect: Roger Anger

Client: Auroville community

Contractor: Built by Aurovillians

Year of Completion: 1976

Area: 278 m$^2$

The inspiration and guiding force for the foundation of the experimental community of Auroville was the utopian vision attributed to the Mother, the late spiritual leader of the Sri Aurobindo Ashram in Pondicherry. The difficult challenge of translating that vision into a unified architectural concept fell to a French architect and devotee named Roger Anger. His Sanskrit School typifies the peculiar curvilinear idiom he devised for the key institutions and sacred buildings of the settlement. Ferro-cement and terra forming, exploited for their low-tech ease of construction and sculptural freedom, are the basis of this sensual, somewhat dated futuristic design.

The school has a simple, atavistic *parti*. Several small classrooms, a library and service spaces surround a small womb-like void filled with greenery and water. The swelling walls exclude the exterior environment from the inward looking sanctuary of study. One crosses a tiny moat to enter the building. Reflected light and breezes moistened by evaporation wash into the interior through elliptical apertures at floor level.

1. View from the garden
2. Interior courts, detail
3. Internal landscaping
4. Wall and fenestration detail

*Overleaf*
5. Entrance
6. Plastic forms in ferro-concrete

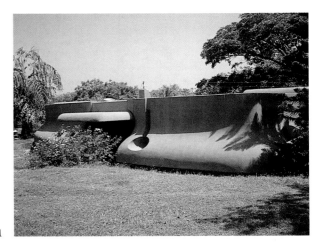

1

2

3

4

5

6

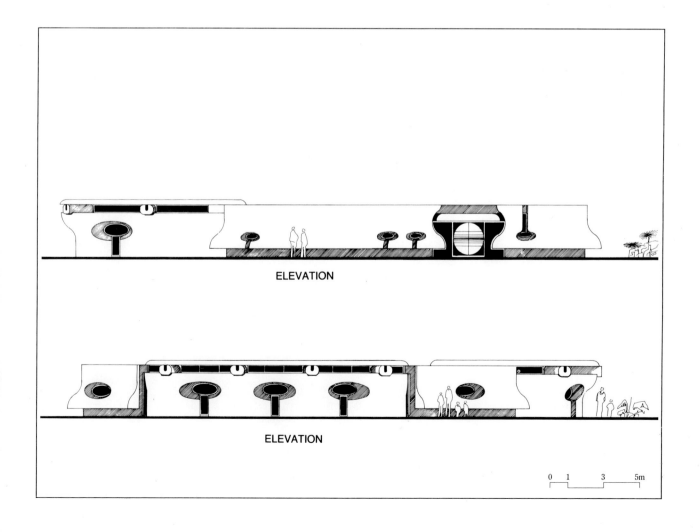

ELEVATION

ELEVATION

0   1      3      5m

## Miraonevi Nivas, Architect's Own House, Auroville

## Architect: Poppo Pingel

Contractor: Built under direct supervision of the architect

Year of Completion: 1981

Area: 120 m$^2$

A common theme in much of what is termed as 'alternative' architecture today is reunion and harmony with nature. This is particularly prevalent in the building efforts of Auroville where the relative isolation of most structures has encouraged a sympathetic integration with the rural setting. However, the literate craftsmanship of this architect's own dwelling debunks the premise that a natural, environmentally sensitive building must derive its form from the local vernacular, or alternatively, from the geometry and raw substance of nature itself. Miraonevi Nivas (Wind House) derives from a Japanese tradition of architecture and landscape. That special sensibility for the elements of landscape and construction is translated into a house of superior architectural merit at one with its transformed Indian milieu.

The architect likens the roof to the protective wings of a bird. A large simple gable with deep overhangs of 1.5 metres shelters the open spaces below from rain and sun. Thin, undressed granite posts locally available at little cost are integrated with timber and some precast concrete elements in a diaphanous post and beam structure. Granite members are also employed — with practicality and eloquence — as lintels over the broad door and window openings that pierce the whitewashed masonry portion of the structure. Floating platforms extend from the living space over the intensively landscaped gardens surrounding the home.

1. Expressed granite and timber elements
2. Weave of house and garden
3. Hybrid construction
   *Overleaf*
4. Verandah
5. Interior, upper study
6. General view from rock garden

1

2

4

5

6

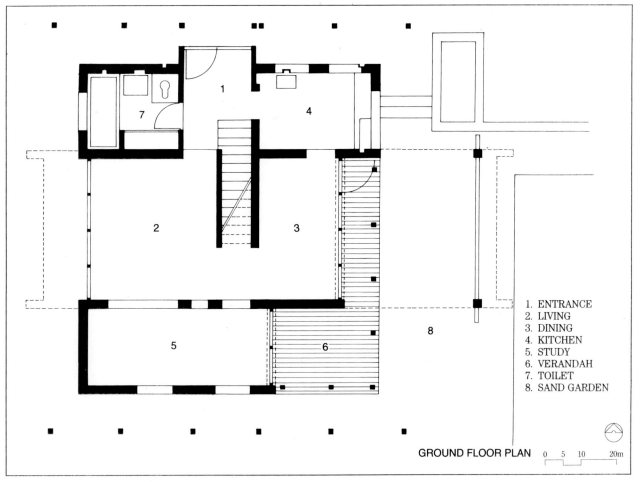

1. ENTRANCE
2. LIVING
3. DINING
4. KITCHEN
5. STUDY
6. VERANDAH
7. TOILET
8. SAND GARDEN

GROUND FLOOR PLAN    0  5   10    20m

## Hirvai, Architect's Own Cottage, Nadhawade

## Architect: Shirish Beri

Builder: The architect
Year of Completion: 1983
Area: 112 m$^2$

A sense of self-sufficiency and architectural harmony with the environment are the magically realized intentions of this idyllic retreat in the lush jungles of coastal Maharashtra. The immediate natural environment is the source of inspiration for this project. The architect's two-hectare site is a lush patch of field and jungle endowed with a certain spiritual auspiciousness in the form of a pair of ruined temples. The house is designed around several huge trees that partially conceal the building beneath their foliage, integrating it harmoniously with the surroundings. Inside and outside spaces are woven together with flamboyant planting. A bathing pool is excavated next to the entrance patio and veranda with its various platforms. A charming studio mezzanine and ground level bedroom have large shuttered windows that open on to exotic jungle views. During construction, an effort was made to optimize the use of locally available building materials. The foundation of the main building uses stones obtained when digging the bathing pool; load-bearing walls are of native laterite stone; woods from the surrounding forest are used for the roof and the mezzanine; floors are of mud with a cowdung plaster finish. Only the roofing is of a commercial material — red clay tiles. The large veranda that serves as the entrance and principal living space of the house is supported on carved wooden columns of 55 centimetres diameter that were recycled from a nearby village temple. The structure, with its pyramidal roof and rustic stonework and carpentry was self-built with the help of local villagers at a final construction cost of under Rs. 120 per square metre (approximately $ 10.00) in 1982.

The architect's design extends to the landscape and its ecology. His orchard has more than 40 species of trees including cashewnuts, cacao, coconuts, lemon, litchi and mangoes, planted along with more than 90 types of flowering shrubs to enhance the beauty of the garden. Smaller open areas are used to grow vegetables, herbs and necessary cereals for personal consumption. Harvests are large enough to support the builder and his family and within the next few years the orchard is expected to produce cash crops. To complete the ecological cycle, animal and human waste is digested in a bio-gas plant to produce cooking fuel. The effluent from this process is used as a fertilizer.

1. Interior view
2. General view from bathing pool

## Day-Care Centres, Dakshinpuri and Seemapuri, New Delhi

Architects: Vasant and Revathi Kamath
Grup India Limited (design associates)

### Client: Delhi Development Authority

Consultants: Patel and Associates (structure)

Contractor: Eastern Construction Corporation

Year of Completion: 1982

Area: N/A

The Delhi Development Authority, among other large municipal corporations in India, has adopted the policy of resettling the population of inner city slums on large suburban tracts of serviced land. The day-care facilities provided here include supervision and primary education to the children of low-income working people who commute daily to the city from these colonies on the fringes of Delhi. The building at Dakshinpuri is organized around a 3 x 3 metre planning module in a matrix of chambers, corridors and courts. The order and proportion of spaces is determined by a basic masonry vernacular. Modules are interconnected by semicircular arches which provide a visual continuity through the interior. The manipulation of different levels gives each module an identity which separates small group activities such as story-telling and games without using walls. The modular order extends to the semi-protected outdoor areas on the south side of the building and the entrance pergola on the north. The building is of two storeys. The ground floor is used for the activities of infants'and toddlers; the upper level for older children in primary classes.

The detailing of the exposed brick exterior is decoratively handled. Rain water is channelled off the roof through traditional *khal-parnalas* (tiled reveals) set into the wall. A corbelled band of brick gives the structure a cornice. Flat and semicircular arches frame small unglazed windows enclosed with wooden shutters. The dimly lit arched spaces within have a cave-like feeling which is loved by the children.

Two similar day-care facilities in the Seemapuri resettlement colony are also small buildings built of brick. The first structure at Seemapuri is covered with four barrel vaults of varying lengths, placed next to one another and supported on intermittent brick peers and a continuous load-bearing perimeter wall. The vaults on both edges are interrupted in the middle, they form courtyards on either side and bring light to the central space. In the second instance, larger interior chambers were required for combined activities. To span this large space, brick domes spanning a square of four modules were used, they give an entirely different character to this building. The domes were economically built without any shuttering using the traditional, mason's techniques revived by Hassan Fathy — the Egyptian champion of low-cost vernacular architecture 'for the poor'.

1. Entrance through exterior court.
2. Semi-enclosed teaching space..
3. General view, Dakshinpuri centre.
4. Day-care at Seemapuri with parallel vault construction.

*Overleaf*
5. Facade view, resourceful use of traditional brick details
6. Children at play
7. Arched portico

6

7

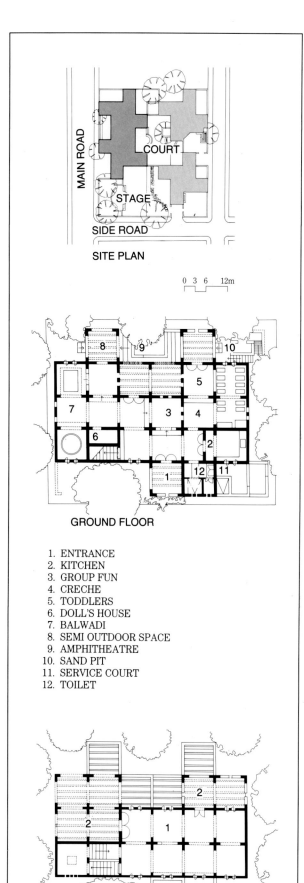

SITE PLAN

0  3  6    12m

GROUND FLOOR

1. ENTRANCE
2. KITCHEN
3. GROUP FUN
4. CRECHE
5. TODDLERS
6. DOLL'S HOUSE
7. BALWADI
8. SEMI OUTDOOR SPACE
9. AMPHITHEATRE
10. SAND PIT
11. SERVICE COURT
12. TOILET

FIRST FLOOR

1. PRIMARY CLASSES
2. PERGOLA COVERED TERRACE

0  1  2    4m

Centre for Development Studies,
Trivandrum

Architect and Builder: Laurie Baker

Client: Centre for Development
Studies

Year of Completion: 1975

The architecture of this academic complex was conceived as a demonstration of economically responsible building practices. It demonstrates, however, that sumptuous and expressive design need not be inhibited by frugality.

A library tower and administrative block are set at the highest point on the site. The tower — a multistoreyed affair, polygon in plan with a pagoda roof — crowns the hill with low-rise teaching spaces and faculty offices clustered about its base. A second group of structures comprises the guest and student quarters and their common dining facility. Staff housing is located on the outer edge of the campus on an elevated patch overlooking a wooded corner of the site. The complex has been gradually expanded, each phase serving as an opportunity to refine a vocabulary of low-cost materials and techniques. Simple brick, wood, concrete and ceramic tile are rendered in an unusual, sometimes beautiful, new light. An appealing and cost effective application of concrete, for instance, is the so-called 'filler slab'. Filler construction substitutes reject clay tiles for expensive concrete in the lower tension portion of a reinforced concrete slab where the steel performs the only structural role. The economy of this method is complemented by the aesthetic coffered effect.

The library and the adjoining classroom and administration spaces are arranged around a pair of small irregular courts. The tower is built of porous brick screens with glass fixed behind to keep out birds and dust. The circulation spaces that ring the inner courtyards are also enclosed with brick screens. The building has several whimsical staircase turrets and oblong milling areas between offices and classrooms. The intertwining levels and stairwells around the entrance lobby and library accommodate the natural slopes of the site. Consistent detailing brings harmony to free-form planning with no spatial standardization, at least in the original structures. However, the most recent

addition to the group with the drab regularity of its straight sash windows is somewhat distracting.

The main residence for male students is a conventional single-loaded hostel block. It is commodious, however, and each room has its own bathroom. The two-storeyed building stands on a slope, its rooms opening on to verandas facing the downhill side. The long corridor that runs the length of the building is enclosed and supported by undulating brick screen similar to the brick *jali* of the library tower. The modulated sunlight that filters into this whitewashed passage is enchanting.

The dining hall, a tiny well-proportioned structure, is planned as three long bays supported by load-bearing brick walls and pilasters carrying sloped filler-slab roofs. One bay is interrupted by an open-to-sky reflective pool. The structure is well integrated with the adjacent guest house and its garden. It functions as a link between hostels and the guest house, bringing students and visitors together in a less formal setting.

The guest house is an exquisite retreat with several private rooms and a common lounge. The conventional materials of the other campus buildings are enriched with special carpentry and textile work to enhance domestic comfort. The hand of an architect schooled in the arts and crafts tradition is apparent in the thorough and intimate details of the interiors. The manipulation of floor levels, built-in furniture and spatial proportions is a wonderful fusion of Oriental and English conceptions of domestic space.

1. Full scale construction study
2. Water court

   *Overleaf*
3. Library tower
4. General view from approach
5. Brick *jali* detail

3

4

5

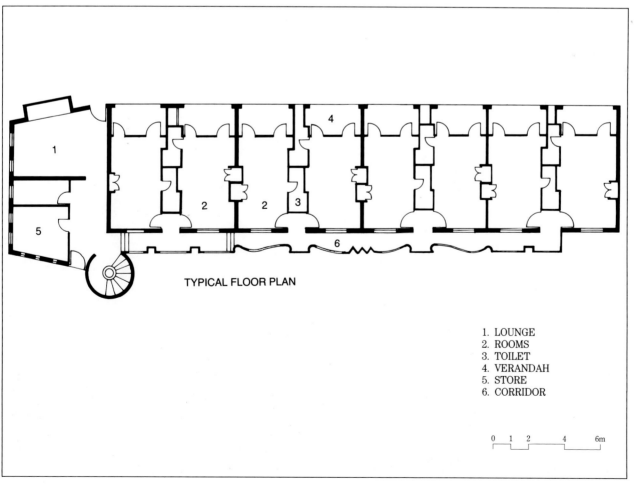

TYPICAL FLOOR PLAN

1. LOUNGE
2. ROOMS
3. TOILET
4. VERANDAH
5. STORE
6. CORRIDOR

0  1  2    4    6m

129

## St. John Cathedral, Tiruvalla

## Architect and Builder: Laurie Baker

## Client: The Syro Malankara Church

Year of Completion: 1973

Area: 1140 m$^2$

The Roman Catholic Church has been an important part of South Indian culture for several centuries, especially in the State of Kerala. However, the design of this provincial cathedral is one of the few attempts, past and present, to break away from the massive Baroque prototype of church architecture first imported by Portuguese missionaries. The revolutionary edicts of the sacred Vatican Council of the early 1960s encouraged a reinterpretation of many traditional forms and ideals with a view to encouraging a more personal involvement of the worshipper in the church. Implicit in these changes was a call for more accessible and culturally appropriate church architecture. With its circular plan and tent-like wooden roof, this Keralan cathedral is a response to the modern Vatican; an attempt to design an indigenous church type.

The building is sited in a semi-rural context adjacent to a main road. One enters it through a large brick gateway proceeding down a broad set of stairs to the level clearing in a grove of coconut trees in which the building nestles. An adjoining church hall designed by a different builder shares one edge of the space. The building is complemented by these surroundings though it stands as an object in space that has little to do with the actual architectural context of nearby Tiruvalla.

The structure is built of local materials. Stone piers are the main load-bearing elements. Non-load-bearing brick infill, as intricate grill work, allows air and light to filter into the hall. Long plywood trusses, assembled at the site, spring from the piers to meet at the apex of the structure about 25 metres above the floor. The clear-span conical roof, which has a collar of dormer windows, is crowned with an impressive cross. The sizable structure was erected with innovative ad hoc engineering with the help of unskilled labourers and local parishioners.

The interior experience is inspiring, moody and reminiscent of soaring Gothic spaces. The building is a fine example of the architect's arts and crafts training in England. This is well displayed in the Ruskinian harmony between the tectonics of the construction and the decorative and textural development of the architecture; a creative collaboration between the architect and various artisans who were responsible for some excellent iron and stained-glass work.

1. Entrance gate
2. Soaring wood truss vault

    *Overleaf*
3. Louvered wall construction
4. General view
5. Decorative metal work

1

3

4

5

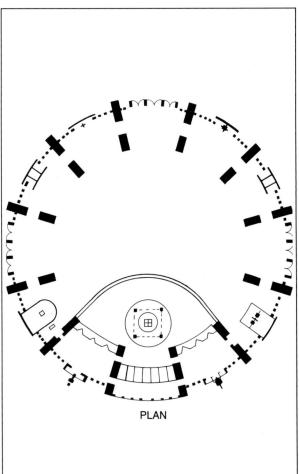

PLAN

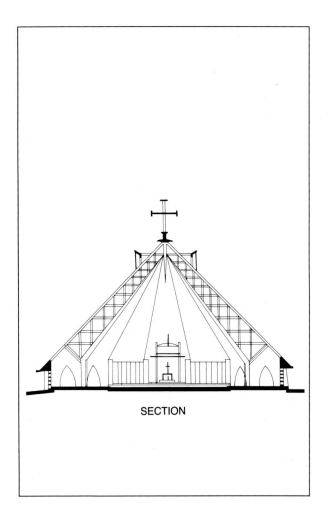

SECTION

Christav Chapel, Kottayam

Architect and Builder: Laurie Baker

Client: Christav Ashram

A modest structure, this chapel reinterprets the elements of traditional church form in a free and inventive fashion. Conventional materials have been adapted to some unusual forms in a building that responds exquisitely to both its tropical locale and its spiritual function.

The chapel serves a small spiritual community in the hills of Kerala. It is sited at the crest of a gentle slope surrounded by coconut palms, casuarinas and rows of eucalyptus trees. The open pavilion-like structure floats on a delicate frame above a raised plinth, its open sides protected from rain by the overhang of the roof. The building has a distinct nave and apse. A low horizontal space roofed with a concrete filler slab defines the nave. An aisle of short concrete columns, reminiscent of the pillared halls of classical South Indian temples leads to the altar under the circular apse. This space is supported by V-shaped wooden struts that integrate it with the trusses of the conical roof. The half-height parapet wall and tiered contour of the floor slab gently modulate the contained space drawing attention to the altar at the centre of the apse.

1

1. General view from the east
2. Apsidal truss supports

*Overleaf*
3. Roof cone above alter
4. Nave with filler slab ceiling
5. View of apse

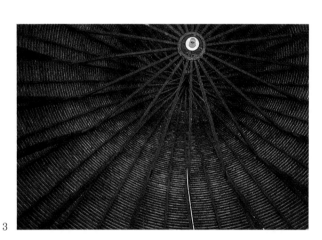

3

4

## Prototype Low-Cost Housing, Trivandrum

## Architect and Builder: Laurie Baker

## Client: Bishop of Trivandrum

Year of Completion: N/A

Areas: 58 m$^2$ (workshop); 25 m$^2$ (reception)

The Catholic diocese of Trivandrum commissioned the construction of these two structures to demonstrate low-cost design and building techniques to church volunteers working in rural areas. Simple but expressive, they have a good visual presence. Their construction is sufficiently straightforward and they can be easily replicated by rural craftsmen without any technical input. The traditional form of the structures is ideally suited to village housing but they have proved adaptable to other functions as well. One demonstration hut now serves as a reception office, the other as a workshop.

The present workshop structure has three bays of equal length, each approximately 2.5 metres wide. These short spans are bridged with collar trusses economically fabricated from small wooden elements. A part of the central bay has no roof and forms a courtyard. Living and kitchen spaces are kept to the front, sleeping areas to the rear of the bays. The other demonstration structure is square in plan, divided in two unequal sections. The first is narrower, used as an entrance porch in front and kitchen at the back. The other wider section of the layout is the living and sleeping area. The structure is covered with a pyramidal wooden roof clad with clay tiles. The living and kitchen areas in both the hut plans relate directly to the courtyard and entrance porch respectively. They extend the usable spaces of otherwise small rooms. The expense of glazed windows is avoided and masonry minimized with the practical and decorative use of *jali* wall construction. Adequate light and ventilation is diffused through these perforated brick walls. The humid tropical climate of South India is mild enough not to warrant the use of window shutters during winter. Though the demonstration structures are presently covered with clay tiles it is possible to cover them with coconut thatch which is inexpensive and can be upgraded at a later date.

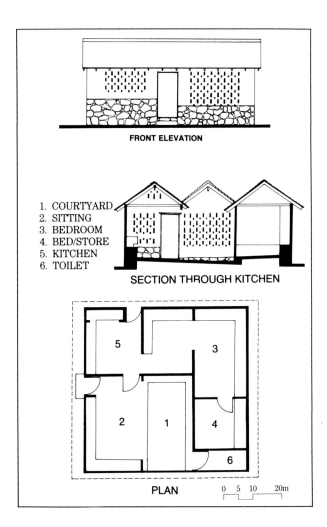

FRONT ELEVATION

1. COURTYARD
2. SITTING
3. BEDROOM
4. BED/STORE
5. KITCHEN
6. TOILET

SECTION THROUGH KITCHEN

PLAN   0  5  10   20m

Experimental hut, presently used as an office

# 4. ARCHITECTURE AND THE MARKET-PLACE

*". . . India is a country of splendour, of extravagance and outward appearance; the Head of a mighty Empire ought to conform himself to the prejudices of the country he rules over . . . In short, I wish India to be ruled from a palace, not from a country house; with ideas of a Prince, not with those of a retail-dealer in muslins and indigo . . ." Viscount Valentia, (c. 1806)[1]*

The Indian middle class was spawned by the economic and administrative transformations brought upon the nation by the British. Today, India is run by technocrats and aspiring business entrepreneurs: the heirs-apparent of the British sahibs of the Imperial Raj. Since Independence, a free and democratic India has been developing on the basis of a mixed economy. The government has assumed responsibility for building the economic infrastructure, a research and development base, and most of the low-profit primary industries. The private sector has concentrated largely on the high-profit, ready-made consumer goods industry,[2] an orientation that has cultivated an increasingly autonomous economic status for the middle classes. Distinguished from the backward, rural masses, the Indian middle class must be regarded as one of the more competitive and accomplished societies in the world today.

Built into the hotels, commercial complexes and middle-class housing developments of urban India are the image and fantasies of this ambitious, upwardly mobile society. The law of demand and supply suggests that this commercial architecture is probably the most direct and truthful expression of contemporary Indian identity that architects have to offer. But the influences that mould this reality are diverse and contradictory: western consumerism, eastern religion, Indian and American cinema, and sentimental nostalgia — not only for rural Indian ideals, but for the imagery and custom of the colonial era as well. New commercial architecture is often modelled after foreign precedents. However, an important transformation is inherent in the process of programming and realizing such projects in the Indian context. Because of the labour-intensive building industry, economic parameters differ considerably, even inversely, from the forces that control real estate development in more industrialized economies. This has inspired some surprising and sometimes flamboyant responses to the demands of popular taste.

Significant among the forces that have shaped the ideals and tastes of the middle class is the imagery of Indian movies. Radio, television and the printed media are allied image-makers as vehicles for the promotion of consumerism and corporate India's idea of progress. The Indian film industry is the largest in the world but virtually all its output is geared to the home market according to standard formulae for marketable content: the glamour and sentiment of an idyllic past, kings and queens and fairy-tale romance. The story-line is stereotyped: boy meets girl but their love and ultimate marriage are complicated for a couple of hours of melodrama by the gulf of wealth, status and traditional intolerance that separate their respective families. The happy ending is inevitably resolved by guarantees that life will be carefree and full of riches ever after. This fantasy and nostalgia is a counterpoint to the value system of a conservative society that continues to adhere to religious tradition and tightly knit family structures.

## ARCHITECTURE AS STAGE-SET: HOTELS

Film producers play up the differences between rich and poor with decadent scenography, schmaltz and glitter. In this sense, contemporary Indian cinema is reminiscent of the Depression era escapism of Hollywood. The large luxury hotels of India are fantasies on much the same order — architectural extravagan-

zas that set the stage on which the middle-class urbanite may escape into the surreal opulence of movie-land.

India's quintessential dream hotels are literally the palaces of royalty. Many of the splendid castles and palaces of the former princely rulers of India have been successfully converted into commercial resorts. But many new hotels are being built all the time and these must depend on their own fabricated splendour.

The Welcomegroup, a major hotel chain in India, adopts a different architectural theme for each of its hotels. Historical and regional colour further animate the ambience. The Mughal Hotel in Agra, part of the Welcomegroup chain, is a skilfully choreographed piece of popular architecture that manages to juxtapose the catchings of the ubiquitous Grand Hotel with the exotic theme of the imperial Mughal court. In sight of the exquisite monuments and gardens of the Taj Mahal, the hotel is outwardly subdued, half concealed in its own extensive grounds. Ostentation is constrained to the marble-everything lobby with its huge chandelier and sweeping grand staircase; the classic, film producer's image of luxury. But the real attraction is the salubrious Mughal gardens that comprise the heart of the low-rise, court-oriented hotel complex. The rich geometry of intensive waterworks and terraced planters, and the soothing gurgle of fountains are the charm of this manicured oasis amidst the heat and dust of Agra. Though compressed and popularized to the resort function of the hotel, the court garden convincingly recalls the imagined hedonistic delights of the Mughal emperors in their verdant palace gardens.

Fig. 4.1
Portuguese vernacular building from Goa with metal rain protection.

The populistic intentions of hotel design are revealed most flamboyantly in large urban centres, especially in Delhi, where the need to provide international-class accommodation is coupled with the desire — on the part of the foreign visitor — for a taste of the exotic offerings of India. Delhi's new World Trade Centre and its adjoining hotel block is a particularly bombastic example. A classic modernist tower-and-podium based building is transfigured, with a copious confection of sandstone, into a high-rise castle of fantastic scale. The building stone and the Mughal genesis of the ornamentation contribute to the contextual gestures of the architecture. But this image is again transformed with an exuberant art deco vision that emerges from the sculpting of the large volumes and the jazzy opulence of interior features, such as a huge marble wall of water in the lobby and the detailing of ornamental metal work, floor finishes, elevator doors and lighting. The Babylonian delirium of the concept — emphasized by the sight of hundreds of drone-like labourers methodically building this structure — reminds one of the epic film productions of Cecil B. de Mille.

Among the noteworthy new hotels of India — and certainly the most colourful — is Cidade da Goa, a beach resort in the former Portuguese colony on India's humid south-west coast. Goa was established by Vasco de Gama more than five centuries ago. Even today it maintains a magical blend of Latin and Asian culture; the unique ambience that Charles Correa has attempted to capture in this enchanted retreat for the sybaritic diversions of foreign tourists and upper-class Indians. Cidade de Goa is perhaps the most literal conception of hotel as a stage set that one could imagine. The illusion Correa creates is of an Iberian village. His set pieces toy with the lingering ghosts of the Portuguese, a collage of architectural and painterly vignettes. Fantasy is the device, spirit of place the objective, and vibrant colour and painted illusions play a seductive role in the experience. The actual construction of the buildings and the intrinsic order of structure, services, space-types and geometry, which have been significant design determinants in Correa's other work, are largely sublimated by the artifice.

Traditional Portuguese architecture is a vernacular of sun and dry heat. It was not ideally suited to resist the torrential rains and humidity of tropical Goa when Portuguese colonists transplanted their culture to India. In the process of acclimatization, they learned to apply temporary weather protection elements to their buildings during the summer and the monsoons (Fig. 4.1). Correa's hotel refers almost too directly to the Portuguese sources of Goan architecture, failing to acknowledge this important prosthetic dimension of the customized Indian version. It fails climatologically, and remains somewhat alien in a cultural sense. However, one suspects that this quality of the surreal is intended in part as a caricature of the colonial regime it evokes. It is a measure of the irony and caprice of popular taste that this gentle pastiche celebrates a socio-political anachronism that, less than three decades ago, India was compelled to defeat by force.

*Opposite page*
Street view (see p.172)     141

Fig. 4.2
The Windsor Manor Hotel.

Fig. 4.3
Typical Circuit House.

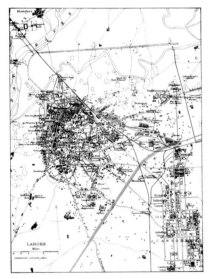

Fig. 4.4
Plan of a cantonment.

The painful stigma of colonialism appears to be rapidly vanishing in Indian society. Hoteliers, developers and architects sensitive to commercial trends have begun to exploit a burgeoning revival of appreciation for the pomp and splendour of the British Raj. Welcomegroup's Windsor Manor Hotel in Bangalore (Fig. 4.2), a recent addition to that chain, is an intriguing indication. Though a fully serviced, centrally air-conditioned building in its 'back of house' operation, the hotel presents itself as an eighteenth century neo-classical palace in the modified tropical style of the British East India Company. It is uncanny how matter-of-fact this regeneration of the past is posited; the gesture astoundingly complete and genuine by comparison with the Post-Modern historicism typical of the West in the 1980s.

## THE BRITISH LEGACY: CANTONMENTS AND BUNGALOWS

The quotation at the opening of this discussion was a defence for the lavish Government House that Lord Wellesley, Governor of the British East India Company, had built in Calcutta at the turn of the nineteenth century, primarily for his own use. Ultimately, he was forced to resign his post, accused of abusing the wealth of the Company. Meanwhile, British rule in India was consolidated and prevailed for almost 150 more years. The wealth and grandeur the British Raj attained in that period is recorded in the magnificent legacy of colonial architecture it left behind. These buildings embody not only the dreams of Empire but the major socio-economic changes that brought India into the present.

Early British architecture in India tended towards the neo-classicism of Georgian England. Later, in the nineteenth century, the Gothic revival and its British Indian hybrid, the so-called Hindu-Gothic became the predominant styles for larger public buildings. The final phase of monumental construction was in the early decades of this century when Edwin Lutyens and Herbert Baker laid out the new capital at Delhi. The most impressive of the Raj buildings were erected in Madras, Calcutta, Bombay and New Delhi, cities which emerged as focal points in the colonial relationship with Britain. But a network of more mundane building types supporting district level administration, was developed throughout the subcontinent. Omnipresent among these was the circuit-house (Fig. 4.3).

Circuit-houses, or *dak* bungalows as they were popularly known, were built for the travelling officials of the Raj. These outposts were instruments for controlling the vast territory of India by establishing a physical presence in remote areas. In the interests of both expediency and authoritative consistency, these buildings evolved an elegant and simple form which also provided comfort and protection against a severe climate. With slight variations in design the standard type functioned well in either hot-arid or hot-humid weather, the two predominant climates of India. Drawing from the climatological rationale of traditional Indian buildings, the bungalow employed a huge roof and porous substructure to screen the suns's rays and allow the wind to penetrate. Flexible walls were produced by changing the classical loggia into a veranda with wider intercolumnation and altered proportions.[3]

The successful proliferation of the bungalow was determined as much by the planning practices of the British Indian military as it was encouraged by the basic practicality of the building type itself. By the late eighteenth century the British controlled such large areas of India that a new military strategy was devised to deploy troops and artillery flexibly and rapidly. This had profound consequences on the pattern of new settlements. Troops were no longer concentrated in the centres of towns, but located alternatively in permanent camps known as cantonments on their peripheries.[4] This strategic policy mirrored the romantic nostalgia for the rural life which had begun to gain popularity in early nineteenth century England. The first commercial reflection of this was the London garden suburb of St John's Wood commenced in 1820. In India, the growth of an analogous suburbia in the British cantonments was the beginning of a radical alteration in the spatial structure of urban India. Military engineers laid down spacious new streets lined with avenues of trees and orderly compounds of officers' bungalows, staff barracks, clubs and other facilities. The verdant expansiveness of these settlements represented a huge contrast to the congested bazaars and high density of indigenous urban housing (Fig. 4.4). This enforced a sense of social separation between the European and native communities. This racial consciousness was gradually supplanted by the class consciousness of the new Indian elite whose suburban villas eventually incorporated the military cantonments in their garden-city sprawl. The historic and inherent exclusiveness of the suburban domicile has undoubtedly preserved the popular appeal of the detached bungalow in modern India, even if most of the urban population cannot hope to ever live in one.

Although the suburban ideal has survived the socio-political evolution of Indian society over the past century, the architectural image of the ideal bungalow has considerably changed. With the forward-looking euphoria of the immediate post-independence era, the traditional colonial style bungalow lost its popularity among upper-class Indians. Private citizens were as eager as the Indian government to express their progressive spirit and the strident new image of modern architecture quickly found its way into the style-books of the residential development market. But inept adaptations of such prototypes as Le Corbusier's Shodhan Villa — showy bastardizations of architectural form with little deference to climate, durability and beauty (Fig. 4.5) — have tended to mutilate the idyllic image of the simple bungalow in a garden.

Fig. 4.5
Ugly modern bungalow.

## REVIVALISM

While India remains committed in spirit to the project of social and technological modernization, the 'post-modern' backlash against the uglier excesses of modernist culture is as keenly registered in the popular tastes of India in the 1980s as it is in contemporary fashion and design worldwide. Recently, a clear trend towards the revival of traditional imagery — including the colonial tradition — has begun to appear in the commercial housing market. The classic British bungalow, with its aristocratic sobriety, and its authoritarian connotations softened by time, once again appeals as the exclusive alternative to a residential landscape glutted with ersatz modern housing. The efforts of developers to create a faithful, genteel rendition of cantonment-style housing as demonstrated in a recent widely advertised development near Delhi (Fig. 4.6), are invariably targeted at only the wealthiest home buyers. Competition and the grossly escalating cost of land in larger urban areas has priced even the upper middle class out of the most exclusive developments.

Fig. 4.6
The Garden Estate Housing, New Delhi.

A limited collectivization is the strategy by which innovative architects are attempting to fulfil the suburban ideal of the upper middle class. An absurdly literal interpretation of this strategy is Yashwant Mistry's whimsical megastructure constructed in Ahmedabad in 1987; a tower of single family bungalows, red tiled roofs and all, stacked up almost twenty storeys high (Fig. 4.7). However, considerably more sober offerings have also been marketed with success to the same clientele. In several notable housing developments in suburban Ahmedabad, the design partnership of Kamal Mangaldas and Devendra Shah has demonstrated an uncommon sensibility for the necessary balance between commercial, sociological and aesthetic criteria in the design of middle-class housing. The successful strategy of this firm suggests that the evolving prototype for such housing must have higher levels of amenities, such as private gardens, adequate room for parking, round-the-clock water supply, and a budget permitting even a community swimming pool — features that are missing in traditional urban housing. At the same time, commercial success with a tradition-minded clientele can depend on familiar appearances. Many of the potential home buyers for whom Mangaldas and Shah's projects are designed are migrating from dense inner-city housing because of overcrowding and the growth of their extended families. The characteristic grouping of row houses in double-loaded private streets that Kamal Mangaldas has used in several different developments, is deliberately analogous to the *pol* (cul-de-sac street) housing typical of old Ahmedabad. The familiar inward-looking type is expanded proportionately to provide greater space and privacy while preserving a traditional sense of security and community. The architectural expression employed is a gracious fusion of colonial classicism and Gujarati vernacular as the two were married in the nineteenth century manor houses of Ahmedabad's textile magnates — an appropriately contextual image of well-mannered success.

Fig. 4.7
Bungalows in the Sky, Housing by Yashwant Mistry, Ahmedabad.

Mangaldas and Shah have done much in their architecture of recent years to promote and refine the revival of the colonial idiom. Their most interesting project in this regard was the commission to expand and recondition a family recreation club in suburban Ahmedabad. The original facility, a group of nondescript block and concrete structures built in the sixties, was grievously lacking in the desired social atmosphere of a club. Playing upon the conspicuous name of the institution, the Rajpath Club (Kingsway Club), Mangaldas successfully fused

Fig. 4.8
Vikas Minar, New Delhi.

Fig. 4.9
Life Insurance Corporation Office, New Delhi.

and transformed the scattered amenities into a tidy compound characterized by a festal vocabulary of colonial elements and ornamentation: extensive verandas, balconies and colonnades, large overhanging tile roofs, delicate wooden balustrades and polychromatic stone floors. The popularity of these revivalist renovations is indeed ironic. Less than forty years after the departure of the British from India — in the very city that was the base for Gandhi's freedom struggle and that later invited Le Corbusier and Louis Kahn to set the standards for its contemporary civic image — colonial architecture is fashionable once again.

The British involvement in India is being re-evaluated; inevitably it must be seen as an integral part of the Indian cultural heritage. For the present, however, the renewed appreciation of British-Indian architecture has not extended beyond the symbols and ornamental ambience of the Raj. What 'sells' in the up-scale housing and hotel markets of the 1980s is the nostalgic imagery of a bitter-sweet past. The more universally applicable principles that gave coherence and rationality to architectural design in the colonial era are, so far, ignored.

## CORPORATE ARCHITECTURE

In the domain of contemporary corporate architecture, the influence of the substantial legacy of British commercial buildings in India is absent, even at a superficial level. In the major business centres the desire to project a progressive and powerful image for big corporate clients has driven architects to design high-rise office towers of anonymous Modernist pedigree. The colonial architectural heritage of cities such as Calcutta and Bombay, embodies the vital commercial activities that made them great. But that older infrastructure has been allowed to decay, unappreciated and violated more and more by the imagery of a brave new world.

To build high continues to enjoy a potent symbolic appeal with both clients and their architects. Vikas Minar (the Tower of Progress) is the isolated high-rise structure that houses the Delhi Development Authority. It could not be a more demonstrative monument to the simplistic ideal that higher is better (Fig. 4.8). But this tower and most high-rise office structures in India suffer from the limited sophistication of their concept and execution. The Indian building industry does not have access to the quality of prefabricated materials with which the cool and elegant lines of international style corporate architecture are derived.

A generally positive tendency in contemporary Indian design has been to assimilate and transform, to some degree, received precedents and imagery. On the other hand, the colossal office complexes designed by Raj Rewal are successful examples of imported architectural style selected for its appropriateness to the rugged methods by which buildings are constructed in India. However, these structures remain alien in their urban context.

In the design of large office buildings for the Life Insurance Corporation of India (L.I.C.), Charles Correa has attempted to address the question of context while maintaining a commitment to the corporate client's need for a distinctive architectural identity. The huge L.I.C. office building on Connaught Circus in New Delhi is, for all intents and purposes, a confident restatement of the aggressive geometries and taut surfaces popularized by corporate image-makers such as I.M. Pei and Kevin Roche who dominated international corporate architecture in the 1970s. Correa runs into difficulty in defending the contextual compatibility of this fragmented block of stone and mirror-glass amidst the neo-classical order of Connaught Place (Fig. 4.9).[5] Although the architect has conceived a dramatic image suitable for the public use of this building — grand stairs and raised plazas under an over-sized parasol soaring high above — the sheer scale of the gesture shares none of the familiar intimacy of the adjacent classical shopping arcade.

A more responsive if less challenging corporate architecture is found in certain regional offices of the big banks and corporations where the smaller scale of operations allows for an easier integration of the new with the existing. The network of branch offices for the Life Insurance Corporation of India designed by Jal Gadhiali are a solid and consistent example. Balkrishna Doshi's regional headquarters for the Central Bank of India and Hasmukh Patel's similar office block for the Dena Bank, both in Ahmedabad, are exploratory exercises towards a compact building type designed to be inserted into an established urban context. In essence, the components of these buildings are the tower and podium of the classic corporate prototype. In context these are reduced to proud but unobtrusive proportions where the base element connects with the existing urban fabric and the tower sits back as an autonomous object in space. Even at this small scale, however, the marriage of the corporate tower with an urban order is difficult.

## ARCHITECTURE AND THE CITY

Conspicuously absent in new corporate architecture in India is the sensibility for the natural symbiosis of building and urban form that was developed so extensively in the old commercial cores of British built cities. These cities are still distinguished by their colonial town planning and many impressive nineteenth and early twentieth century office buildings. Whereas the imagery and symbolic value of this least celebrated domain of the British legacy are somewhat ambiguous, the highly principled civic decorum ingrained in this architecture offers the contemporary architect valuable cues to design. The ramifications of these principles extend, obviously, to the form and order of the urban environment.

The dense agglomeration of Victorian public and commercial buildings in the Fort area of Bombay is richly varied in style and treatment. But it is a remarkably coherent urban experience, woven together by the topological consistency of the built form and, most importantly, a sense of complicity and convention in the harmonious accommodation of the public realm by the architecture. Individual buildings contribute to a greater urban order; they stand together forming a continuous street facade and a uniform profile. The important programmatic requirement, the question of image, is answered in the articulation of the facade and volumes, sometimes to flamboyant degrees. At the foot of these buildings the device of the continuous pedestrian arcade brings beggar and businessmen together in a weather protected public space that harbours the life of the street.

In the midst of a proliferating urban chaos the office and commercial buildings of the colonial era provide a model for a coherent consolidation of the Indian city through the forces of commercial development. However, architectural imagery is easier to absorb than the principles of good design. In the marketplace, which is and shall be the most active field of architectural endeavour for years to come, the power of the isolated statement is bound to prevail if so allowed. In housing and hotels such free-wheeling fantasy may be acceptable for these are, after all, every man's castles. Office buildings and large-scale commercial developments are another and more public matter; the architect shares the challenge and the responsibility to shape these forceful interventions to the order of the city.

**NOTES:**

1. Philip Davies, *Splendours of the Raj, British Architecture in India 1660-1947*, Dass Media in association with John Murray, London, New Delhi, 1985. p. 68.
2. Pran Chopra, *Uncertain India, A Political Profile of Two Decades of Freedom*, MIT Press, Cambridge, Massachusetts, 1968. p. 118.
3. Sten Nilsson, *European Architecture in India 1750-1850*, Faber and Faber, London, 1968. pp. 176-178.
4. Davies. op. cit., pp. 103-132.
5. Charles Correa, *Charles Correa*, Mimar, Singapore, 1984. p. 100.

1. Restaurant and lobby from internal court

*Overleaf*
2. Landscaping, internal court
3. Corner detail, view from outer gardens
4. Formal water garden
5. Terracing and planting, internal court

## Mughal Sheraton Hotel, Agra

Architects: ARCOP / Ramesh Khosla,
Ray Affleck
Design Group – Ajoy Choudhury,
Ranjit Sabikhi, Kiran Gujral, Anil
Verma

Landscape Architect: Ravindra Bhan
Client: Indian Tobacco Company
Limited

Consultant: Gherzi Eastern

Contractor: G. S. Luthra and Sons

Year of Completion: 1976

Area: 18,000 m$^2$

A regal informality, as might have been enjoyed by the Mughal emperors in their palace gardens constitutes the thematic ambience of this international resort hotel. The tourist attractions of Agra include two of the greatest architectural treasures of India — the Taj Mahal and the royal complex of Fatehpur Sikri. The experience of these monuments was closely considered in the design of this hotel. However, the architects wisely avoided any attempt to copy their unique forms or details. Emulation is limited to the interlocking courtyard organization of the plan and the intensive Mughal style landscaping of these spaces. The hotel is located to the south of the Taj with a view of the monument, however, many of the guest rooms look inward on the garden courts. There are three quadrangles, one of which contains an outdoor swimming pool. Landscaping is organized on an informal geometry of squares and octagons. Flowing water channels, pools and fountains, subtle level changes buttressed with planters and formal rows of trees and flowers graciously fuse the Islamic garden tradition to a modern context.

The buildings themselves are unimposing with their low-rise brick construction. The massing and articulation of the architecture, internal planning and the overall concept of an inward-looking garden hotel, closely resemble another hotel built in Montreal a decade earlier by the Canadian members of this international design team.

146

1

2

3

4

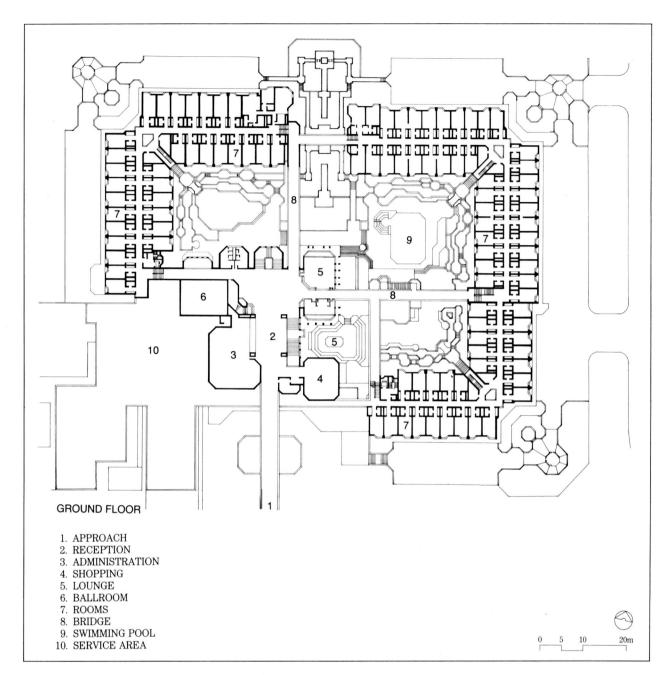

**GROUND FLOOR**

1. APPROACH
2. RECEPTION
3. ADMINISTRATION
4. SHOPPING
5. LOUNGE
6. BALLROOM
7. ROOMS
8. BRIDGE
9. SWIMMING POOL
10. SERVICE AREA

0    5    10         20m

5

Bharat Hotel Complex, New Delhi
**Holiday Inn**

Architects: Debashish Guha –
ARCOP Associates

## Client: Bharat Hotel Limited

Consultants: C.P. Kukreja and Associates
(structure), Nirmal Gupta and Associates
(mechanical), S.G. Deolalikar (services)

Contractors: Uttam Singh Duggal and Sons, and
Competent Construction Limited, New Delhi

Year of Completion: 1988

Area: 100,000 m²

This complex, comprising a high-rise luxury
hotel, condominium office tower and world trade
centre, is a significant addition to the already
burgeoning skyline of New Delhi. The hotel tower
climbs 18 floors above a 5-storeyed podium of
lobbies, shops and restaurants. The trade centre —
a merchandise mart for Indian export goods — is
an autonomous extension of this podium. A tall
narrow atrium divides the two halves. Smaller,
open-to sky light shafts penetrate the heart of the
trade centre block forming elegant hard-surfaced
courts. Decorative paving patterns and the stylized
articulation of the exterior stone cladding are
attractive selling points of this commercial
development. The condominium office building, a
smaller separate structure, was built as the first
phase of the development to finance the remainder
of the project. This building is to be connected to
the whole by landscaping and a stone pergola in
the updated Mughal idiom with which the whole
complex has been rendered.

All three buildings are clad with sandstone in
variations of yellow and red reminiscent of the
many Mughal monuments in and around Delhi.

Uncommon attention to the detailing of this
material distinguishes this project from the many
other recently constructed hotels and commercial
buildings in Delhi to which stone veneers have
been applied. Though the architecture makes no
pretence of being traditional, the modern structure
is not merely sheathed with stone, but modulated
and embellished with considerable image-making
abandon. In a chunky, mannered interpretation, the
*chattri* (delicate pavilion-like element) so prevalent
in Mughal architecture) is a recurring motif used
for such key elements as the giant *porte-cochère* of
the hotel and the entrance porch to the trade
centre. In their most evocative application, *chattris*
crown the crest and corners of each building
volume lending them a castle-like profile. Such
ornamental panache extends to the hotel lobby
with its green and white marble detailing. The
design marks a departure from the Brutalist phase
of contemporary Indian architecture. However, this
confectionery retort to exposed brick and concrete
is ultimately less exquisite than it is extravagant in
its quality of detail.

1. Main gate and *porte-cochere* beyond.
2. Monumental "chatri" on banquet hall facade.
3. *Porte-cochere* from the north.

1

2

3

## Ashok Yatri Niwas, New Delhi

Architect: Jasbir Sawhney and Associates, Design Team: Jasbir Sawhney, Saroj Sawhney and Dinesh Sareen.

Client: India Tourism Development Corporation Limited

Consultants: Stup Consultants Limited, New Delhi (structure), Rajeev Sethi (interior design)

Contractor: National Building Construction Corporation Limited

Year of Completion: 1982

Area: 23,000 m$^2$ (565 hotel rooms)

1. Facade detail

   *Overleaf*
2. General view
3. Corbelled massing optimising natural ventilation and views
4. Interior, typical guest room

Ashok Yatri Niwas is an economy hotel developed by the India Tourism Development Corporation to provide moderately priced accommodation on a large scale for visitors to the national capital. It is located in the immediate vicinity of several high priced hotels and Connaught Place, the main commercial hub of New Delhi. The need to optimize the use of the real estate and maintain the image of this prestigious neighbourhood were important criteria defining the design problem. Another challenge was to create a cosmopolitan ambience, sufficiently urbane to meet the expectations of middle-class Indians, yet appealing in its sense of place to foreign tourists.

Minimum service and maintenance requirements are the basis of economy in the design and operation of this 565-room high rise. Despite its height, circulation corridors are exposed to the elements at every level in such a manner that guest rooms can be cross-ventilated without mechanical air-handling systems. Public corridor spaces are treated as the building exterior, detailed with coarse building stones for wall surfaces and paving. These durable finishes, in red and yellow sandstone on alternate floors, resist abuse and bring a warm texture and colour into the public areas of the building. Corridor lengths, space use and structure were optimized by the geometric analysis of room shapes, and their crystal-like clustering. The porosity of the resulting configuration admits light and air to the circulation spaces which interconnect, in turn, through common light wells. The guest room interiors are rustic but tasteful. Furniture is built-in, raised platforms for beds, writing tables and lighting concealed in niches. Small terracotta plates are set in walls as decoration. The floors are precast reinforced concrete panels finished in earthen colours. A low rise office and shopping annexe cradles a small plaza adjacent to the hotel planted with several mature trees — a pleasant civic gesture.

According to the architect, the costs were about 40 per cent that of a comparable 3-star hotel. Unfortunately, some of this frugality has backfired. The cheap tile applied directly to the structure as exterior cladding (contrary to the architect's advice) is not performing well and threatens to fall off with the strains of thermal expansion and humidity. Another cost-cutting tactic was to minimize the number of elevators causing long waits for hotel guests. There is, however, a provision for additional lifts and the installation of air-conditioning in the design of the vertical services.

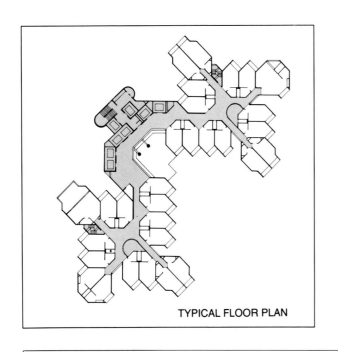

TYPICAL FLOOR PLAN

2

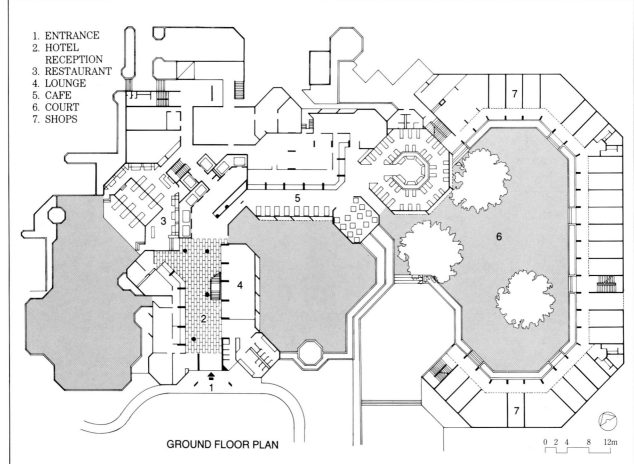

1. ENTRANCE
2. HOTEL RECEPTION
3. RESTAURANT
4. LOUNGE
5. CAFE
6. COURT
7. SHOPS

GROUND FLOOR PLAN

0  2  4    8    12m

3

4

Cidade de Goa, Dona Paula, Goa

Architect: Charles Correa

Client: Indian Tobacco Company
Limited

Contractor: N/A

Consultants: N/A

Year of Completion: 1982

Area: N/A

Fantasy and luxury go together in this enchanting beach hotel. The resort was designed for a hotel chain that markets itself on the theme of India's various historical and regional subcultures. The lush tropical milieu of Goa, with its colourful legacy of Portuguese colonial rule, provides the inspiration for an architectural stage set steeped in imagery and illusion.

The resort occupies a private cove shaded with coconut trees. A steep escarpment rises behind, ensuring privacy and a sense of escape from the outside world. This feeling of isolation is exploited in a loose, unconventional interpretation of the hotel programme that is distinct from both urban prototypes or the 'Club-Med' image of a grass-hut paradise under the palms. The concept of this resort lies somewhere between — a contiguous grouping of low-rise masonry structures modelled on a small town. A vibrant palate of earth tones and pastels and a series of illusionary murals by poster painters from the Bombay movie industry enrich and distort the impression towards the surreal. One is reminded of Dali and de' Chirico. The buildings belong to the hot dry climates of Latin Europe with their flat roofs and deep-cut openings in thick plastered walls, (a serious problem, incidentally, when it comes to Goa's torrential monsoons).

The architecture is a sequential experience. The hotel is approached by road from the top of the escarpment. One passes through a gateway and down a slope on to a plaza; a town square-like space with painted facades. Casual, life-size mannequins depicting Vasco de Gama and friends welcome guests — with a little tongue-in-cheek — to the lobby reception area. This is a breezy open loggia that overlooks the garden and swimming pool and the Taverna bar-lounge beyond. The guest rooms extend in two loosely parallel ranks along the crescent of the beach. The steep slope staggers the floor levels dramatically in such a manner that every room has an excellent view of the water. Rooms are reached through an adventurous network of stairs and undulating passageways that branch off into a sequence of linear courtyards between the two blocks. Restaurant and conference facilities adjoin the entrance plaza for easy public access.

Attention to many image-making details, such as the use of cast-iron benches and street lamps as urban furniture on the entrance plaza, and the re-use of salvaged elements from older colonial buildings, has enhanced the visual delight of the project. However, the conceit teeters on the edge of kitsch. The fantasy wears thin with the total artifice of internal spaces, such as the Alfama restaurant, that have no interplay with the exotic splendour of the natural environment.

1. Private terrace overlooking ocean

*Overleaf*
2. Taverna bar
3. Lobby
4. Entrance loggia overlooking pool
5. General view from the beach

2

3

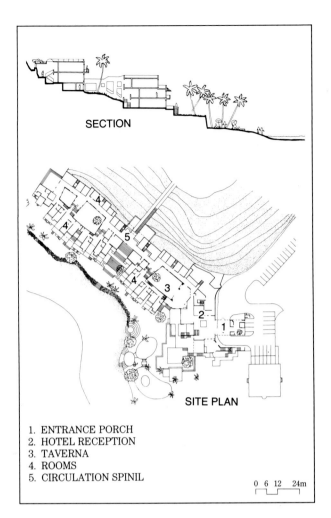

SECTION

SITE PLAN

1. ENTRANCE PORCH
2. HOTEL RECEPTION
3. TAVERNA
4. ROOMS
5. CIRCULATION SPINIL

0  6  12    24m

4

5

Prainha Cottages, Dona Paula, Goa

Architect: Ralino de Sousa

Client: Palmar Beach Resorts

Contractor: Premier Builders, Panaji

Year of Completion: 1985

Area: 1350 m$^2$

These tourist cottages are only subtly distinguished from their colloquial Goan surroundings. The architecture lies in details; an exaggerated but eloquent articulation of massive timber and masonry construction. With a sense for the picturesque, the architect has sited the row of cottages on the sloping crest of an abandoned stone quarry. Thick, slightly battered walls appear to grow out of the rock, eroded away into windows and verandas, crowned by large red-tiled roofs. These appear to float above the heavy white walls from which they are visually divided by a deep reveal in the timber structure. The projecting purlins of the roof and all wooden doors and shutters are highlighted with bright tropical colours. The cottages overlook a coconut grove to the sea beyond. Deep verandas are set under the roofs with large louvered doors that extend these spaces into the guest rooms. Exposed rock terraces adjoin some verandas where the contour of the cliff edge permits.

1. Picturesque roof lines and massing
2. Articulated wall and roof construction
3. General view through coconut grove

1

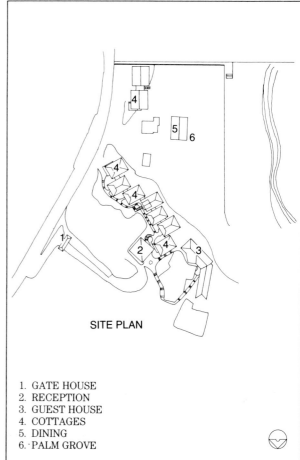

SITE PLAN

1. GATE HOUSE
2. RECEPTION
3. GUEST HOUSE
4. COTTAGES
5. DINING
6. PALM GROVE

2

3

## Rajpath Club, addition and extensions, Ahmedabad

## Architects: Kamal Mangaldas and Devendra Shah

## Client: Rajpath Club Private Limited

Contractor: N. G. Patel

Year of Completion: 1986

Area: 2000 m²

The metamorphosis of this family recreation club is intriguing. Built in the 1960s in a nondescript rendition of the International Style, its members came to regret the club's lack of atmosphere. The present commission to expand the facilities included a mandate to renovate and transform the existing buildings. Towards this reincarnation, and keeping the name of the club in mind, the newly appointed architects decided upon a concentrated reuse of British colonial imagery. The first phase of the renovation saw the addition of a 12-room guest wing. This was laid out perpendicular to the main structure along the end of the swimming pool to give a sense of enclosure to the complex. The rooms are organized on two levels with garden patios at the back and verandas overlooking the pool in the front. Phase two saw the expansion of the main clubhouse. This included the addition of verandas, a banquet hall, card rooms and related services. The new and renovated buildings are roofed with heavy red-tile gables that have restored a visual unity to the club compound. The delicate woodwork of brackets and balustrades and other built-in furniture adds to the neo-colonial ambience.

1. Pool side facade, renovated banquet hall
2. Pool side colonnade
3. View through colonade from residential block towards the clubhouse.

1

2

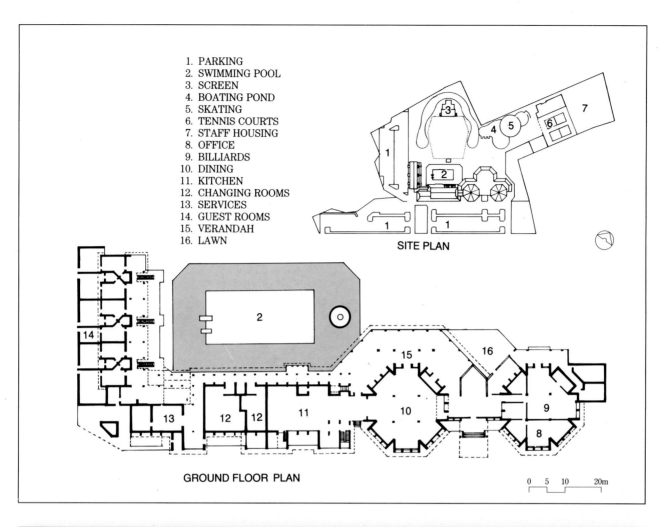

1. PARKING
2. SWIMMING POOL
3. SCREEN
4. BOATING POND
5. SKATING
6. TENNIS COURTS
7. STAFF HOUSING
8. OFFICE
9. BILLIARDS
10. DINING
11. KITCHEN
12. CHANGING ROOMS
13. SERVICES
14. GUEST ROOMS
15. VERANDAH
16. LAWN

SITE PLAN

GROUND FLOOR PLAN

0  5  10    20m

## Sanjay Park Housing, Ahmedabad

### Architects: Kamal Mangaldas and Devendra Shah

### Client: H. K. Construction

Contractor: H. K. Construction

Year of Completion: 1985

Area: 6000 m$^2$ (31 units of 190 m$^2$ each)

The familiar attempt of real estate developers to generate profitable sales with inexpensive building methods and a gloss of sentimental tradition is evident in this example of housing, built with considerable more taste than is the norm. The development anticipates an inevitable increase in the density of neighbouring housing projects. Row-type dwelling units are packed closely together and turn in on a long semi-private compound much like the so-called *pols* (cul-de-sac streets) that have evolved in the older quarters of Ahmedabad as an efficient, low-rise, high-density pattern of distribution for urban housing. A gate marks the entrance into the compound and the gesture is repeated in the graceful rhythm of the arching metal lamp standards that span the street space. In an effort to support a sense of community and self-sufficiency a cluster of amenities have been made available at the top of the site. These include a tube well, water tower and a yet to be completed clubhouse and swimming pool, — suburban substitutes for the neighbourhood temples of the old town.

SITE PLAN

1. HOUSING UNITS
2. COMMON OPEN PLOT
3. CHANGING ROOM
4. PLANT ROOM
5. WATER TANK
6. SWIMMING POOL

0 5 10 20m

The units are narrow-front row-houses — 3 storeys high, 15 metres long and 5.5 metres wide. Each is penetrated by a central shaft similar to the internal courtyards found in the *pol* houses of old Ahmedabad. Living, kitchen and dining spaces are arranged around this on the ground level; the sleeping areas are above. The void is roofed over but provides adequate ventilation with the stack effect generated by the clerestory windows at the top. The upper floors of the housing are stepped back to create private terraces off bedrooms that can be used for outdoor sleeping in the summer. Each unit has a front garden and a rear kitchen yard. The exterior is finished with sand-coloured aggregate plaster. Sloping red-tiled canopies provide sun and rain protection. They also unify the development with their characteristic domesticity.

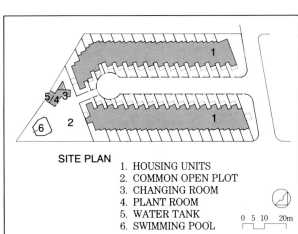

1. Private gardens addressing internal street
2. Living room
3. General view
4. Typical unit

3

4

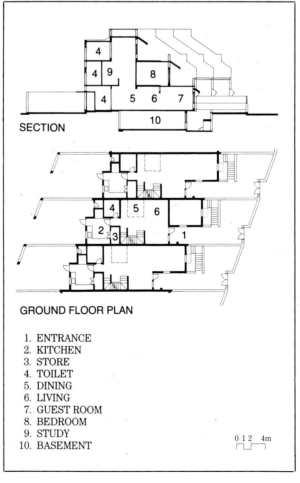

SECTION

GROUND FLOOR PLAN

1. ENTRANCE
2. KITCHEN
3. STORE
4. TOILET
5. DINING
6. LIVING
7. GUEST ROOM
8. BEDROOM
9. STUDY
10. BASEMENT

0 1 2    4m

165

## Gulmohur Luxury Housing, Ahmedabad

## Architects: Kamal Mangaldas and Devendra Shah

## Client: Gulmohur Housing Colony

Contractor: Navratna Builders, Ahmedabad

Consultants: N/A

Year of Completion: 1986

Area: 18 units, 256 m$^2$

1. Side elevation
2. Kitchen yard
3. Typical entrance gate to individual unit
4. Decorative carpentry, entrance gate

Autonomy and architectural identity are some of the prestigious hallmarks in a housing market governed by the high cost of land and services. But these ideals often end in failure in the eclectic jumble of over-sized houses that tend to be built. The Gulmohur Housing Estate is small (18 units), elegant upper middle-class development that strikes a compromise between the home buyer's ideals and orderly, more economical planning principles that have been successfully applied to housing developments of a less exclusive character. Stylistically, the architecture reverts to the grand manner of colonial classicism; a solid, acclimatized vein of the expression that reflects the fusion of certain European 'tastes and manners with the lifestyle of the Indian upper classes. The late nineteenth and early twentieth century manor houses of Ahmedabad's textile magnates are the source of this imagery; a formal masonry reinterpretation of many details and features found in the old wooden *havelis* (large city houses) of Gujarat. A sense of stylish grandeur is achieved by aligning the housing on a formal avenue graced with a canopy of gulmohur (*Delonix regina*) trees. A series of elaborate wooden gateways, derived from the traditional form and symbolism of the *darwaza* (gate), open on to each private compound. These dwellings are semi-detached to optimize the amount of open garden space per unit, while maintaining the impression of large stately bungalows. Paired units have been joined into one unit in a few cases where members of a joint family have occupied each half. The units are spacious yet efficiently planned; bedrooms and living spaces expand on to various verandas and balconies. Finished basements — an unusual feature in Indian domestic architecture — open on to their own sunken terraces. Backyards are equipped with washing areas and servants' facilities adjoining the kitchen.

3

4

## Regional Offices, Central Bank of India, Ahmedabad

### Architect: Balkrishna Doshi – Vastu-Shilpa

### Client: Central Bank of India

Consultants: Mahendra Raj – Engineering Consultants India (structure)

Contractor: Gannon Dunkerley and Company

Year of Completion: 1967

Area: 11,000 m²

1

In established trading centres such as Ahmedabad, intensive commercial pressure on tight parcels of real estate has spawned a specific archetype for medium-rise commercial buildings. This proud, if diminutive bank tower is a precedent for several corporate buildings that have come up more recently in this city. The type is characterized by its classic division into podium and tower elements, often complemented as it is here by a third element, a small auditorium. The podium occupies almost the entire plot area; a low-rise infill that ties the building into the existing streetscape. The office tower stands above and apart from the eccentric base and its function as the public banking hall. The regular form and proportions of the tower emphasize the structural rationale of high-rise architecture. The building is rectangular in plan. Mechanical services and vertical circulation are concentrated at the rear because of the constraints of the plot. These rise in a prominent shaft up the back of the structure. The

volumetric organization of elements is distinctly anthropomorphic; the service core analagous to a spinal column, the tower the head and the podium the shoulders of the architectonic creature.

The architect's earlier involvement in the design and execution of Le Corbusier's Ahmedabad commissions — particularly the Mill Owners' Association — is a prevalent source of inspiration and a fluent facility with Corbusian form is apparent. The cast *in situ* concrete construction is not particularly well finished but rendered elegant by the decisive proportioning and articulation of structure and surfaces. The large balconies on the main south facade and floor-to-ceiling sun-breakers along the east and west exposures protect glazed surfaces from direct radiation. The tower is topped off, in Corbusian fashion, with a large roof terrace. But this is interpreted in a more classical, almost Grecian manner as a noble double-height loggia.

1. Partial view of the tower from Sidi Saiyed Mosque
2. Expressive *brise-soleil* and loggia of the office tower
3. View from the street

168

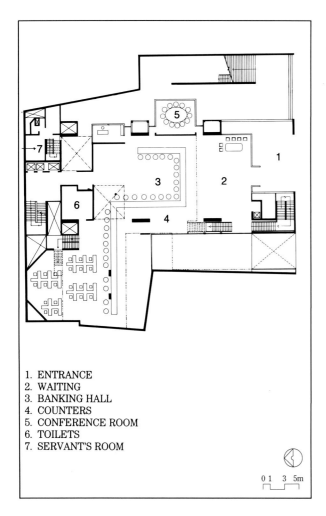

1. ENTRANCE
2. WAITING
3. BANKING HALL
4. COUNTERS
5. CONFERENCE ROOM
6. TOILETS
7. SERVANT'S ROOM

0 1  3  5m

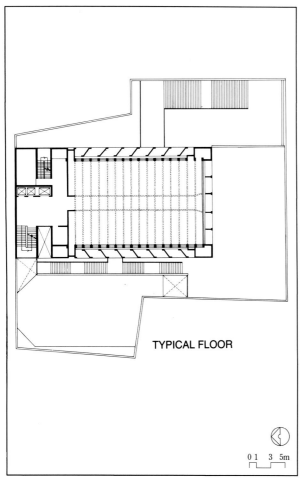

TYPICAL FLOOR

0 1  3  5m

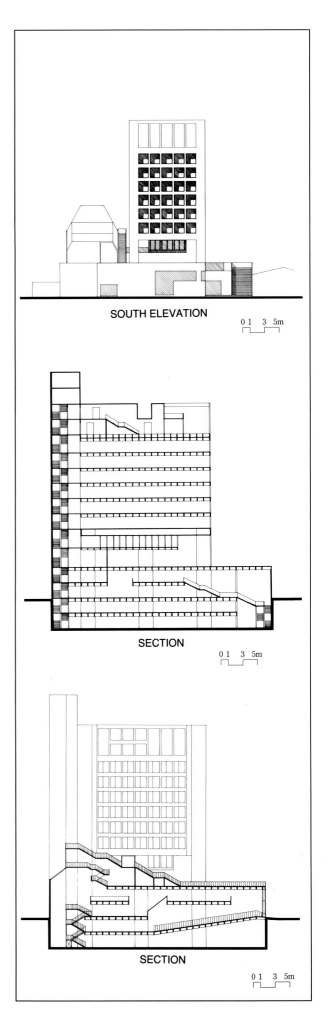

SOUTH ELEVATION

0 1  3  5m

SECTION

0 1  3  5m

SECTION

0 1  3  5m

## Dena Bank, Regional Office Building, Ahmedabad

### Architect: Hasmukh C. Patel

### Client: Dena Bank

Consultants: Vakil-Mehta-Sheth (structure), S. K. Murthy (services)

Contractors: Rajesh Builders and H. K. Builders

Year of Completion: 1982

Area: 6800 m$^2$

The Ahmedabad headquarters of the Dena Bank has its precedent in the Central Bank's Ahmedabad offices designed by Balkrishna Doshi. The programmes of the two buildings with their hierarchical division between an office tower and the public banking facilities at street level are almost identical. Variations in the design of the Dena Bank stem from different site conditions and the need to create a distinctive identity for the corporate client. Although the site is long and narrow, the environs are comparatively suburban, dominated by trees rather than a dense wall of buildings. The office tower recedes from the street, set back on a wedge-shaped podium. A row of neem (*Azardirachta indica*) trees shades the casual entrance plaza that leads into the banking hall. The public is invited to ascend a grand staircase onto the podium. An auditorium, slung beneath the office tower, is accessible from this upper terrace.

The monolithic concrete construction of the building is unusually well finished. The narrow, deep-set fenestration of the wall surfaces presents a variation on the image of security traditional to the architecture of banks. This severity is relieved, however, by the curious face-like incision of windows on the narrow street facade, which reinforces the anthropomorphic massing of this building.

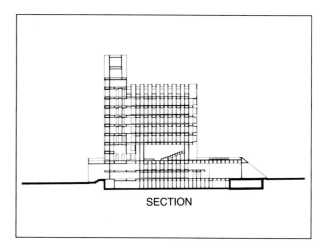

SECTION

1

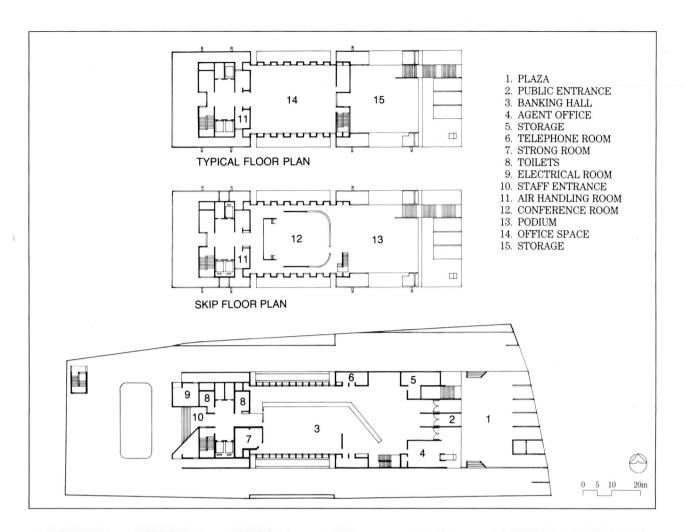

TYPICAL FLOOR PLAN

SKIP FLOOR PLAN

1. PLAZA
2. PUBLIC ENTRANCE
3. BANKING HALL
4. AGENT OFFICE
5. STORAGE
6. TELEPHONE ROOM
7. STRONG ROOM
8. TOILETS
9. ELECTRICAL ROOM
10. STAFF ENTRANCE
11. AIR HANDLING ROOM
12. CONFERENCE ROOM
13. PODIUM
14. OFFICE SPACE
15. STORAGE

0    5    10         20m

# 5. EMERGING ARCHITECTURE

The role of the architect in Indian society will continue to expand in the coming years. The wealth of new architecture emerging in the 1980s reflects this widening mandate and the maturity of the profession after a half century of search and experimentation.

The demand on India's construction industry is steadily increasing with rapid urbanization and industrial growth. Government remains the major client. In 1985, 80 post offices, 120 railway stations and 160 bridges were constructed in different parts of the country. In Delhi alone, a measure of the rate of urban expansion was the building of 12 new transit depots in that same year (Fig. 5.1). Traditionally, the job of designing such mundane facilities, and many prestigious public buildings as well, has been the responsibility of central and municipal departments of public works. But that trend is changing. The pressing demand on the system has begun to create a marriage of necessity between independent consulting architects and the various agencies of the formal sector. Enlightened bureaucrats are coming to recognize the virtues of this fresh conceptual input, not only on the plane of aesthetics, but in much broader environmental, economic and social terms. Measured against the legacy of the formulized modernism from which it is emerging, Indian public architecture in the eighties projects new qualities of substance and originality.

Fig. 5.1
Construction in progress, showing the busy skyline.

## ARCHITECTURE AND THE FORMAL SECTOR

The authority of technocrats, primarily engineers, over architectural projects of the Indian formal sector was a practice established by the British colonial administration. Expediency and bureaucratic inertia have preserved this inverted hierarchy to this day.

In the early years of independence a huge demand for new construction was generated by the impetus towards progress and the simultaneous and unexpected need to house millions of Sikh and Hindu refugees from the new Islamic state of Pakistan following its partition from India. In its infancy, the architectural profession — with only a few hundred members, the majority of whom were in Bombay — could play only a negligible role in that building effort. The challenge fell most readily to government engineers of the Central Public Works Department, the powerful and highly organized institution that had authored most of the public buildings and infrastructure during the British era. With its experience and technical resources the Public Works Department could cope with the initial crises more effectively than the independent architectural profession. However, initial logistical success tended to eclipse the issue of architectural competence. The engineer's priorities in design were less holistic than the architect's; his methods more mechanical. He stood as the necessary champion of pragmatism with regard to the nuts and bolts issues of national development. Through its rapidly proliferating sub-cells in the governments of the new States and larger municipalities, the public works organism continued to execute the lion's share of new construction commissioned by the formal sector.

Fig. 5.2
Utilitarian architecture designed by the Public Works Department; example Madras University Buildings.

Curiously, credit is due to these government engineers and the sweeping building programmes they have administered for firmly establishing the language of modern architecture in India. However, their dogmatic adherence to functionalist design has also served to accentuate the obvious failings of that idiom as it has been applied in India.

The Public Works style of building that made its mark on public housing projects and government institutions in the 1950s owed little to the highly developed language of utilitarian 'background' architecture synonymous with British India (Fig. 5.2). The move towards a progressive new image for the developing nation had encouraged the adoption of new construction standards based on the

*Opposite page*
Library block (see p.204)

Fig. 5.3
View of a typical public housing project.

technology of reinforced concrete. The Department of Public Works of the State of Punjab spearheaded the initiative with its appointment of Le Corbusier, Fry, Drew and Jeanneret to build Chandigarh. The image and construction practices exemplified so particularly in the Punjab Capital Project effectively displaced the masonry-based building standards and typology of the colonial Central Public Works Department. In the southern and eastern parts of the country, where Chandigarh was only a remote influence, public projects assumed a less distinctive but equally modern appearance in the guise of the International Style promoted by Gropius and Breuer.

The need for a critical interpretation of these contemporary form sources was obvious; it was an impetus to many of the interesting tangents of inquiry that independent architects began to explore in India as early as the 1950s. However, with important but isolated exceptions such as the personal commissions of Habib Rahman in his capacity as Chief Architect of the Central Public Works Department of India, the average draftsmen and engineers in the employment of local government departments were undiscerning with regard to design. Modernity was the national ideal. Masses of government housing and institutional structures proceeded to be built in unquestioning conformity with the prescribed formula for modern construction and planning: reinforced concrete frame, masonry infill and flat slab roof; a strip or screen of concrete sun-breakers over continuous fenestration; a linear, outward-looking order of planning with a spacious grid-determined distribution of elements in the landscape. The commitment to these design elements and images ignored the fact that such an intensive use of reinforced concrete was not economical. Moreover, the thin, flat surfaces of the material was predisposed to form were at odds with environmental conditions in most of the Indian subcontinent — the overwhelming heat of the summer months, the driving wind and rains of the monsoon that penetrate a building virtually parallel to the ground, the endlessly filtering dust, the garbage and birds that are prone to collect on the ledges of a *brise-soleil* (Le Corbusier's buildings have not fared any better in this respect). In public housing projects, above all, such planning negated the in-between realm of weather-protected, semi-private space so essential to the Indian built environment (Fig. 5.3).

The repeated, insensitive application of these building practices over the years has not only compromised the quality of the projects concerned, but in its dreariness the average Public Works Department designed building has undermined the popular appreciation of architecture as a constructive process in the physical and cultural development of the country. A large part of the challenge of getting better public architecture built in India today lies in moving the bureaucracy and the general public to recognize the scope and value of architectural design. In the context of a developing society, leading architects have come to regard their roles as lobbyists and educators as an ethical imperative of their mandate to build.

## EVOLVING PRIORITIES

A change in political agenda over the last decade has considerably improved the receptiveness of Indian government officials to the ideas and expertise of the architectural profession. Environmental issues such as deforestation, erosion, energy and water resources, pollution and urban squalor became a dominant theme in the politics of Indira Gandhi during her later years as the Prime Minister of India. The idea of progress that underlay the development efforts of her father, Jawaharlal Nehru, was supplanted by the urgent need to conserve and upgrade an environment threatened by the onslaught of those earlier initiatives. The conservation of cultural heritage was a parallel to the need to protect the natural ecosystem; the man-made environment needed to be sensitive to both.

These political themes have been institutionalized in a variety of new governmental organizations independent of the Public Works bureaucracy. Agencies such as the Delhi Urban Art Commission and the Environmental Planning and Co-ordination Organization of Madhya Pradesh have been created, since the late 1970s, with the purpose of guiding the physical forces of development towards a more constructive impact on the environment. These agencies readily consult the architectural profession. Through their commissions the quest for regional and cultural identity that has long concerned architects in their academic debates and private practice is now publicly endorsed. Being an open issue, the possibilities for the architectural expression of such identity are not strictly prescribed. New work in this vein remains highly individual, the architecture replete with the idiosyncracies of its designers. The most obvious tactic, to emulate the imagery of a colloquial context, has taken a side seat to more subliminal approaches. Architects pursuing these lines are conscious of the uneasy limbo in which they work; a state of conflict between India's heritage and the society's ideals of progress.

The forum for much of this work is a specific building type: the small academic or vocational institute. Under the patronage of government and semi-governmental organizations, this has emerged as the archetype of mainstream Indian architecture in the 1980s, an idealized microcosm of Indian social and spatial order in which the relevance and meaning of architectural design in modern India can be explored.

\*

Balakrishna Doshi has been an inspired pathfinder in the evolution of this building type. Amidst the impressive roster of large public commissions he has executed over the past ten years, his most convincing example of an architecture suited to an Indian context is his own research foundation and atelier, Sangath. Built on the outskirts of Ahmedabad in 1980, it is the experimental ground for the bold new direction Doshi's work has taken in the 1980s. It is a small and tactful building that effects an ideal balance between the timeless meaning of certain constructed forms and the techniques of their making and maintenance; a magical symbiosis of construction and landscape. One is persuaded that this is a *natural* Indian building showing no overt lineage from either the vernacular or the modern masters who had so explicitly influenced Doshi's styles of earlier years.

Isolated and idyllic, the Sangath scheme lends itself to the criticism that it is an arcadian idea of architecture, irrelevant to the context of an urbanizing nation. But this introspective exercise is an essay on ideas and possibilities for the making of architecture in modern India. Sangath is a polemical statement, pregnant with implications that easily transcend the function and isolation of the building itself.

The principles of Doshi's emerging architecture are not specifically form-related, although his continuing interest in the ceramic-glazed barrel vaults, introduced in the Sangath scheme, has apparently consolidated the basis of a new style. Gestures of contradiction and implication that Doshi employs in his buildings are a subliminal mode through which an indigenous sense is instilled. Architectural form is determined by a simple ordering rationale, such as the systematic collection and shedding of rainwater, or the regular alignment of structural piers beneath a cluster of parallel vaults. In Sangath, the various elements of the building are composed as a loose approximation of an inward-looking traditional compound — but only as an inference, not as an outright description of the type. This design *parti* and its underlying order are eroded by extraneous elements of the landscape and the designer himself who wilfully foils the resolution of the gesture, determined not to be seduced by his own artifice. The principle of contradiction is universal, but a consciousness of the irrational and its visual celebration in Doshi's exaggerated treatment of the sculptural oddities of his buildings would appear to be an especially Indian sensibility. The irrational does not negate reason in this society; the two coexist. For instance, in Gujarat State, which is home to Doshi's practice and some of the most progressive industries and scientific research facilities in the country — many millions of rupees were recently spent to erect a lavish temple devoted to the belief that the earth is flat!

One is charmed, and perhaps distracted by the pastoral aura of Doshi's Sangath. The intrinsic appeal of its vaulted construction is enhanced by the ethical conceit that such forms and their scintillating white finish are the product of a low-cost reapplication of traditional ceramic technology. But Doshi has shown this expression to be more broadly applicable. In the Mahatma Gandhi Institute for Labour Studies, completed in 1985, he has restated that idiom on a larger scale with a decidedly more urban order of spaces and elements.

\*

Anant Raje began to practise independently in the early 1970s after years of work with Louis Kahn. The ongoing expansion of the Indian Institute of Management at Ahmedabad (IIM), that he has designed and supervised since Kahn's death, has been a workshop for his experiments with an increasingly personal

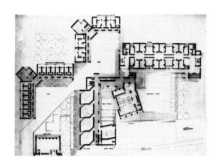

Fig. 5.4
Plan, Indian Statistical Institute, New Delhi.

architecture. Raje works out of a small office on the IIM job-site itself, after the practice of the master builders of the past. A conservative craftsman, his design process is slow and intense; his architecture distinguished by a firm, empirical technique through which abstract formal issues are explored. The work, both projects and buildings, is a continuum of formal ideas unbroken by the constraints of any particular commission. In contrast to the pluralism to which most recent architecture has been subject — in India and abroad — Raje has maintained a remarkably narrow path in the evolution of his style. His work can be read as a whole — a text about the art of building and place-making in which his interventions as a designer have been as an editor reverently honing the turn of phrase.

Raje's most stimulating current work is a group of institutional projects commissioned by various formal agencies, part of the resurgence of government stimulated architectural activity in the eighties. His design for the Indian Institute of Forest Management near Bhopal is a large-scale fulfilment of the themes that have characterized Raje's personal tangent of investigation from his sources in Louis Kahn. Evident in the plan is a romantic urbanity — a loose assemblage of structures woven into a formal unity with a fabric of arcades and screen walls. Buildings are caged and protected within this archael lattice. Volumes and voids of significance in the programmatic hierarchy pronounce themselves with a dominant geometry. They skew and cluster in subtle defiance of the rambling base order; an interplay of objects in space with the urban place contained by this agora-like grouping of monumental fragments on a sloping height of land.

One antecedent of the Forest Management Institute is a tiny campus designed by Raje in 1981. The Galbabhai Farmers' Training Institute is an inward-looking complex where rural management techniques and agricultural technology are taught to semi-literate villagers on short-term internships. It is typical of the hundreds of small institutes in India that serve as symbols of the national development endeavour. The function of the institute is in many ways a parallel to the role of the monastery in most traditional societies, as a beacon of learning and order.

The building speaks of solidity, security and sobriety with its rubble stone walls, concrete arches and lintels marching from pier to pier. The plan delights — while confirming a sense of security — with an elegant curving sweep of wall across the uphill approach. One passes through a contemplative forecourt to the academic compound located at the heart of the complex with the teaching block, dormitory cluster, and the distinctly cloister-like loggia used as the dining space, opening on to it. The elements of the whole coalesce in a rich balance of solid and void, the latter implied more than actually described by any constricting enclosure.

The picturesque idea of unravelling order characterizes a series of Raje's unrealized projects for the Government of Madhya Pradesh. These form the continuum between the Galbabhai campus and the design for the Institute of Forest Management. It is a departure from the austere rigour of his earliest major works as an independent practitioner: the semi-wholesale market complex in New Bombay, and the Indian Statistical Institute in Delhi designed in 1971. The latter was Raje's first independent attempt to handle the typological problem of the institute while he was still involved with Louis Kahn on the Institute of Management. The design of the Statistical Institute is snared in some of the organizational trappings of the Ahmedabad project, most particularly the distribution of hostel blocks in a geometric array about a monolithic faculty core building (Fig. 5.4). Architectural detailing is also faithful to Kahn's spirit of construction, but it is consciously innovative. The result, however, is particularly obtuse. The buildings exhibit a mannerism in that joy of joinery — so essential to Kahn's aesthetic — that approaches the fetish of a cabinet-maker. Fortunately, Raje did not stagnate with those early tendencies. He has evolved away from a preoccupation with technique to an interest in the distinctly romantic qualities of place and architectural memory apparent in his work of the last decade.

The current Madhya Pradesh schemes by Raje recast the elements of form and construction derived from Kahn, in an evocative statement of *genius loci*. The Roman inspiration for Kahn's euclidian abstractions gives way to an empathy for the ramshackled majesty of classical Deccan architecture. The trace of the ruined palace and pleasure gardens of Mandu is almost literal in the swelling arches and layers of thick, perforated masonry with which Raje builds up the designs for his student counselling centre and the Institute of Forest Management, for which his design work began a year later.

Without sacrificing his deeper conviction in the culturally transcendent nature of building, Raje has arrived at his own proposition for a regional architecture in the designs of these government institutes. He has chosen to render the type as a chimera of the courtly graces of a ruined fort-palace. The vulnerability of this picturesque conception lies in its nostalgia — its backward-looking idealism.

By emulating the broken order of a ruin Raje's architectural composition remains, however, open-ended. There are interesting similarities in this lack of resolution to the implied but intentionally uncompleted gestures of traditional organization and form in Balkrishna Doshi's buildings. As a planning model, this open, fragmented trace of order does not necessarily connote decay. It supports the optimistic view that the institutions of a democracy are accessible, they grow, and they evolve.

*

In the typology of the institute Raj Rewal has also made a significant contribution to the emerging architecture of India.

The first phase of Rewal's National Institute of Immunology in Delhi, completed in 1985, is an exercise in institutional housing. Like many Indian institutions, the buildings are isolated on an essentially rural site although the intimations of their form and composition are wholly urban in character.

Rewal's earlier institutional campus — the National Institute of Public Finance — which stands across the road from the Immunology Institute, shares the character and detailing of his large office buildings; an image of corporate strength. The Immunology Institute presents a softer, jazzier humanism that reflects Rewal's experiments with vernacular imagery in his Athlete's Village for the Asian Games of 1982. But it is not simply nor exclusively an option for Tradition versus Modernism. In this exercise, Rewal strikes a balance with a degree of refinement that excels over his previous work.

On a steep, rocky site, three cores of housing form a complementary group. The cores are each distinct in organization and form accommodating a three-tiered hierarchy of scholarly staff. Rewal reduces planning to the elaboration of a simple diagram for each multi-level cluster: a byzantine cross for senior scientists, each arm an outward-looking autonomous element on three sides; a rectangular block for junior research staff, the scheme of the urban *haveli* (inner-city courtyard dwelling) with two external exposures to each unit and access to a common court within; and an inward-looking quadrangle for visiting scholars that could be likened to the form of the *vihara* (ancient Buddhist monastery). These social distinctions in plan are muted by the architect's expressive but homogenizing treatment of surfaces and details. With a Brutalist honesty that overcomes the lax craftsmanship and the sense of pastiche in his Asiad Village, Rewal sculpts, perforates, striates and engraves the built volumes revealing the nature of construction with clarity and eloquence. He doesn't actually show the structural materials but expresses their rationale in the textures and polychromy of the building veneer. Ambiguity between the vernacular and the futuristic is generated by manipulating the evocative profiles of stairways, terraces and *jali*. Red and yellow sandstone, which Mughal builders used to great effect, are crushed into grit and pigment for the aggregate plaster with which structure and infill are delineated.

In spite of his capacity for subtlety, Raj Rewal remains a leading proponent in India of aggressive, big-boned structures. In the 1980s he has added several giant buildings to the Delhi skyline that uphold the youthfulness and optimism first declared in his Permanent Exhibition Structures for the National Trade Fair of 1972. Structure — particularly the challenge of building dynamic long-span structures with labour intensive methods — continues to be the object of his fascination. To keep many hands busy mindlessly pouring concrete, he argues, is a pragmatist's answer to the distressing dearth of skilled craftsmen in the construction industry today. Beyond the hubris of defiant structural gesture, however, this approach to architecture is almost uninvolved regarding the performance it demands from builder and user alike. Buildings such as Rewal's office towers for Engineers India Limited and the State Trading Corporation of India are after-

Fig. 5.5
View of the State Trading Corporation of India's building under construction, New Delhi.

images of the failed vision of the Japanese Metabolists twenty-five years earlier; colossal column-free frameworks that accommodate changing space require-ments and physical abuse with stoic indifference (Fig. 5.5). The paradox is that Rewal's vernacular-inspired housing for the Institute of Immunology articulates a more progressive statement. Where the institute, as a type, is designed as an intimate play of urban textures and relationships, his big urban structures remain violent city-breaking fragments of a mega structural order that could only be fully realized by destroying the urban fabric of past and present.

## THE EMERGING GENERATION

The cultural introspection apparent in recent architectural design in India is in part a function of the Modern/Post-Modern debate. Many young Indian architects are still migrating abroad for further training and work experience. There is a marked commitment, however, to return and practise in India. By comparison with the more and more static state of development in the West, the volatile Indian milieu maintains stimulating opportunities for the architect to explore his own ideas with the strong possibility of implementing them.

Among the architects who have established themselves over the last decade as visible new polemicists are Sen Kapadia and Romi Khosla. A more subdued and introspective professional of note is Leo Pereira. These three represent a new wave of 'foreign-returned' architects who differ in their work, their ideas, and their inspirational sources from the previous generations of Indian architects trained abroad. Although they diverge from each other in their approaches to design, a common denominator in each of their theoretical positions is a prevail-ing belief in the universality of architecture. To build appropriately in India in the present is to exercise creative judgement as to the potential and applicability of the theories and conventions current in contemporary global architecture. The compulsions, crises and the race to modernize that shaped the architect's man-date in the earlier days of Indian nationhood have been superseded today by the dominant roles of theory and design method. The rudimentary deficiencies and demands of a developing society have not vanished, but the emerging generation of architects is trying to cultivate a renewed respect for aesthetic concerns and symbolic criteria in contemporary Indian design.

The Post-Modern critique of twentieth century Western architecture has — perhaps inevitably — found its advocates in India. Romi Khosla and Sen Kapadia might both be pigeon-holed as Post-Modernists, but it would be too facile an assessment merely to trace the gist of their theoretical stances to the debate that has dominated contemporary architectural design in the West since the late 1960s. An educated familiarity on their part with the questions posed by Western polemicists such, as Robert Venturi and Charles Jencks, has encouraged a parallel but independent inquiry into symbols and meaning in modern Indian culture. The Western classical tradition in architecture is acknowledged as a facet of this reality but not as a cultural datum of semantic importance to the Indian psyche (as it has been argued to be with respect to Occidental civilization). The Post-Modern expression in India has, therefore, only an incidental affinity with the image of its American and European parallels. It is the intellectual attitude that is common. The sources of style are as diverse — sometimes equivalent, sometimes contradictory — as is the separate cultural forum to which it responds.

\*

In a battery of articles and manifestos published since the mid-1970s, Romi Khosla has made a call for a conscious questioning of all established precedents for architectural design in India. "Our architecture is not only stylistically incon-sistent, it is totally pluralistic, completely open-ended and yet an inseparable part of the Indian tradition."[1] Khosla is interested in the phenomenon of culture and the iconography of signs and symbols with which architecture supports it. According to him, the impact of communications in the contemporary world is so widespread that the cultural picture of a nation such as India, inevitably includes many facets of relevant imagery from outside its traditional heritage. India is part of a global economic and technological reality that the architect must not fail to exploit. In form and image, however, Khosla believes these contemporary means for building architecture must be tailored to evoke the specific cultural informa-tion inherent in a given programme. This attitude to the making of architecture is, however, highly permissive, with the consequence that his formal ideas vacillate dramatically from one project to the next.

Khosla's written attacks have been aimed not only at the questionable appropriateness of Modernism's cartesian order in the Indian context, but he has also challenged the suitability of Gandhian idealism *vis-a-vis* reliance on traditional technology as the patent answer to the malaise with Western orientations. Khosla is anxious to stifle a chauvinistic ethno-centricity in the conditioned veneration of many of his colleagues for what he terms 'tomb technology'. "Indian contemporary architecture must be freed from the crafts traditions that give it monumentality, permanence, and rigidity."[2] A living architecture responds to the actual socio-economic imperatives of a culture, as it does to its popular imagery and myth. As a chartered accountant who turned to architecture as a second career, Khosla cannot equate the low productivity of traditional, labour-intensive construction practices with the acute demands on the Indian construction industry.

In practice, Khosla creates buildings that are relatively free of idiosyncracy. His architecture suffers, however, from a lack of fluency in the eclectic range of imagery and styles assimilated in his designs. Consistent with his professed antagonism to backward technology, Khosla transforms this found imagery through brick and concrete construction. But the fact cannot be disguised, paradoxically, that his buildings are still largely hand-built.

Khosla's admiration for Robert Venturi is avowed in his frequent employment of the device of exaggerated iconographic form. But he takes exception to the idea of the 'decorated shed': "Architecture is not a structural form modified by the application of iconography (but) iconographic form made out of structure."[3] Khosla's most provocative building in this regard is his school for spastic children, built in New Delhi in 1985. This unusual commission called for a safe, sheltered environment for intelligent but physically handicapped children. In his search for an evocative symbol, the architect turned to the atavistic security of the womb, an idea and quality of form that could address the psychological needs of the users while ergonomically suited to their wheel-chair based movement. The idea is transformed into architecture through the soft embrace of curving brick walls. An oval activity zone, animated by playful ramp configurations, forms a central void within a sombre, box-like volume. A hint of the chamber of discoveries within is promised by peculiar arched openings in the two-storeyed brick facade which shrouds the recessed fenestration. The strange shape of these giant niches is a transformation of a second iconographic schema that the architect has brought into play in his design. They allude to the mysterious portals through which one passes with humility and wonder into the rock-cut temples of ancient India.[4] The womb and the cave are metaphors of each other and of primordial beginnings, awkward but optimistic.

Romi Khosla's architecture is intriguing, but largely an exercise in theoretical concerns that frequently discounts the more conventional but fundamental issue of technique in the art of building. It shares the problem common to most anti-canonical tendencies in contemporary architecture: iconoclastic polemic lacking substance of its own.

\*

Sen Kapadia shares with Romi Khosla a pluralistic approach to design. However, his work reveals little interest in iconography. By resorting to an inventive rather than historiographic mode of rational design Kapadia attempts to break through the stereotypes that have evolved in contemporary Indian architecture through conditioned imagery.

Kapadia worked under Louis Kahn in the early 1970s. He continues to admire the clarity, pride and high aesthetic judgement with which that American as well as his European predecessors — Lutyens and Le Corbusier — were able to build in an alien environment that could provide them only the rudimentary means of construction. He believes their consciousness of the unfamiliar heightened their sensibility for the parameters of the architectural problems that they could work with most confidently: fundamentals such as material, scale, and climate. Kapadia sees a masterful honesty in their efforts that other Indian architects — caught up in the schizophrenic orientations of their middle-class culture — have had difficulty matching in their own work.[5] Kapadia has recognized his own fallibility in this regard and compensates by forcing himself to approach design from unfamiliar perspectives. Architecture has become a game of tests and constraints that he sets for himself to outwit his own pre-conditioned responses to programme and the question of image in the design of a building.

Fig. 5.6
Kushinagar pilgrimage centre, a study, by
Sen Kapadia, architect.

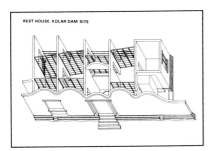

Fig. 5.7
Drawing of Madhya Pradesh Tourist
bungalow, design by Sen Kapadia.

One interesting technique Kapadia relies on is the exclusive use of ax-onometric projections to study the third dimension. He has eliminated the stan-dard elevational drawing from his design method, anxious to avoid an inappropri-ate fixation with two-dimensional facades in an architecture that is rarely urbán; that could be, according to his ideal, merely a fabric of porous construction defining the important place of the garden in the Indian spatial concept.[6] The similarity between the standard axonometric drawing and the oblique projection of space in traditional Oriental paintings has intrigued Kapadia to take this method of perceptual analysis a step further. In his conceptual study (with the National Institute of Design, Ahmedabad) for Kushinagar, a proposed pilgrimage complex for an ancient Buddhist site in northern India, the traditional idiom is used to visualize the scheme. The stylized imagery and vivid colours characteris-tic of the classical miniature paintings of India are employed to evoke appropriate aesthetic values and develop a delicate balance between architectural form and a sacred landscape. Built form is delineated as screens of white 'anti-space' framing and shaping fields of colour (Fig. 5.6).

Kushinagar is one of several interesting projects Kapadia has designed under government commissions. His series of prototypical designs for small Madhya Pradesh government rest houses illustrates the surprisingly eclectic range of expression of which he is capable. Kapadia discards the precedents for this modest, well-developed building type. He re-addresses the programme from two angles: one, the basic rationale, and two, appropriate aesthetics. The first lends a new order to the type that responds directly to climatic and contextual milieu, while the aesthetic consideration determines the formal elements to be invented or retrieved from the cultural repository. Kapadia's designs vary from an overt exercise in village morphology in one scheme, to a strange but delightful composite of neo-classical quotations from the British Indian tradition weaving through a foil of vaguely Japanese screen walls in another scheme (Fig. 5.7).

Among Sen Kapadia's constructed projects are some interesting buildings in Bhopal, the capital of the State of Madhya Pradesh. The Sainik Guesthouse, a hostel for retired military personnel, was designed for a spacious site in a new subdivision of the city zoned for administrative functions. Devoid of any apparent cues from historical or cultural context, the oddly distorted structure is merely a "rational envelope" for the programme, according to the architect.[7] Kapadia lends it a volumetric personality by rotating successive floors of the linear structure about the central service core to overshadow fenestration on the south exposure and concurrently open up verandas toward the north. It is a deceptively complex exercise in the abstracted commonplace.

Regardless of his rationalizations, Kapadia's aesthetic remains challenging and even alien to the Indian context. His buildings for the Institute of Food Science in Bhopal are an especially provocative example. An obtuse expression of purist line and form, they seduce, but fail to enchant with their inexplicable surrealism. The attempt to reinvent a classic type has brought about certain disconcerting innovations in spatial proportions, fenestration and ventilation that tend toward barbarism where the intent was surely to enliven.

A disappointment in the built works of both Sen Kapadia and Romi Khosla lies in their failure to break away from the fixation with architecture as a de-signed object in space. Khosla's buildings are iconographic entities given architectural structure; they want to stand apart with semantic clarity in the manner of a Hindu temple or a Greek-revival courthouse. Kapadia's unbuilt Kushinagar study is a significant attempt to conceptualize an architecture of place. However, his urban projects are self-absorbed sculptural statements that fail to anticipate the order of the city and the morphology of the dense built environment into which they will be absorbed in time. Urban design is a dominant issue in global architecture, but it has yet to make a significant impression on Indian practice.

*

The work of Leo Pereira is a somewhat ironic afterward to a discussion of new architecture in the 1980s. Among the emerging generation of influential younger architects in India, Pereira is an undisguised conservative. In clear and passionate terms his personal version of functionalist architecture affirms, once again, the prevailing vitality of the Modernist paradigm in contemporary Indian design.

Pereira has been practising and teaching architecture in Ahmedabad for the past ten years, quietly earning a reputation as a fastidious craftsman with a series of small-scale residential, church and community commissions. A devout Roman Catholic, his buildings reflect his orthodox respect for rules and a fundamental sense of ethics. Pereira's aesthetic verges on the puritanical in its ascetic white simplicity, but the effect is mellowed by a sentiment for the relationship of the building to the natural environment. The manipulation of daylight and the inter-penetration of site and building are design themes with which he is particularly skilful.

Pereira proclaims no theoretical basis for his work. But a period of graduate studies in Denmark in the early 1970s has clearly imbued his buildings with a Scandinavian approach to modern form and design. This is revealed, in the more technical sense, in the simple, descriptive manner in which materials are assembled and detailed in buildings such as Pereira's own house — a quality suggestive of the joinery of contemporary Danish furniture. The spartan sanctity of Pereira's little church at Gaekwad-ni-Haveli, hints at the direct and compelling inspiration of Aalto and Utzon.

Pereira's quintessential work to date remains his own house. In that diminutive exercise he has brought together his intuitive principles of architecture with his code of ethical convictions. The enthusiasm for this work, among both students and colleagues, is telling, for it suggests a surviving appreciation of *quality* as a fundamental value in contemporary architecture. Novelty and alternative speculation on the theory of design are not, in themselves, automatic virtues.

*

At its finest, the work of the emerging generation of Indian architects complements the long-term efforts of the senior doyens of the profession to shape modern architecture to the demanding parameters of India. In the coming years Indian architects are likely to continue looking for answers to the questions of style, meaning, identity and direction. Inevitably, in a fast-paced, shrinking world, ideas will come from outside the culture as much, or even more so than they can be expected to exude from within. Plurality prevails, the product of many parallel and autonomous efforts, and intimations of any theoretical alliance today are, most likely, only incidental.

**NOTES:**

1. Romesh Khosla, *Journal of Arts and Ideas*, April/June 1985, p. 5.
2. Romesh Khosla, *Tomb Technology and Waves of Slaves*, (unpublished manuscript).
3. Khosla, op. cit.
4. Ibid. p. 34.
5. Sen Kapadia, "Architecture and the Question of Appropriate Aesthetics," *Design*, January/March 1985, pp.24-27.
6. Ibid.
7. Sen Kapadia, *Journal of the Indian Institute of Architects*, July/September 1984, pp.4-10.

## Sangath, Architect's Own Office, Ahmedabad

## Architect: Balkrishna Doshi

## Client: The architect

Consultants: G. N. Tambe (structure)

Contractor: Departmental

Year of Completion: 1980

Area: 473 m$^2$

Sangath, meaning 'moving together', is a rare commission in which the architect, being also the client, was free to explore and realize his most personal convictions. The building and its garden comprise an idyllic work-place for himself and his office staff; it is an essay on environmental design where climatological parameters have been brought into delicate balance with what might be called an existential sense of place. In addition to the design atelier, the building accommodates the Vastu-Shilpa Foundation, a semi-autonomous study cell concerned with human settlement issues in the developing world. Guest quarters for visiting professionals are also integrated in the building.

The structure is domestic in scale, composed as an integral element of a carefully laid-out landscape. It occupies about one-fifth of the 2,500 square metre site. A long barrel vault is the backbone of the composition. This encloses the main studio, set half a level below grade between solid walls. The space is lit through periodic breaks in the vault. The guest quarters and several smaller work rooms are grouped under a pair of raised vaults that terminate the building at the upper end of the site. A porous post and beam structure supports this multi-level weave of spaces. The building frames the garden with a crescent of shallow terraces that softens the gesture to form a small amphitheatre. A third group of spaces, including the architect's office and an informal lecture room, are contained below these terraces.

The vaults are a lightweight composite of materials: cylindrical terracotta tiles sandwiched between thin ferro-cement shells. The carefully rendered underside of the vaults expresses the trace of wooden shuttering. The exterior is dominated by the brilliant white finish of the vaults; a heat-reflecting, waterproof coat of china-mosaic (shards of white ceramic set in cement and polished to a smooth finish after hardening). The collection and shedding of rain water from the vaults through gargoyles and channels to reflecting ponds and ultimately to the garden, is the theme of this poetic yet rational composition.

1. General view from the garden
2. Smooth vault surfaces merging through water course with landscape

*Overleaf*
3. Clerestory illuminating design studio
4. Long vault of the design studio

1

3

4

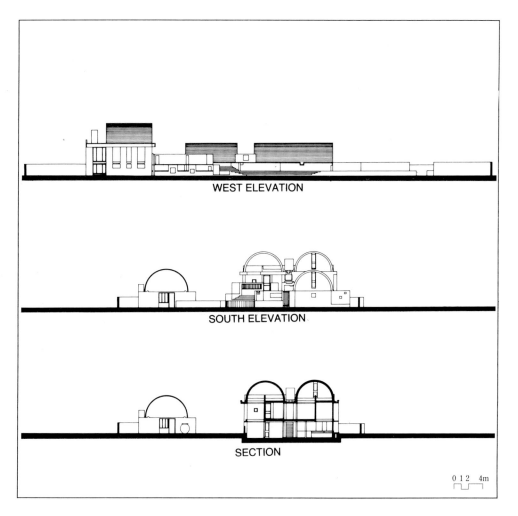

WEST ELEVATION

SOUTH ELEVATION

SECTION

0 1 2 4m

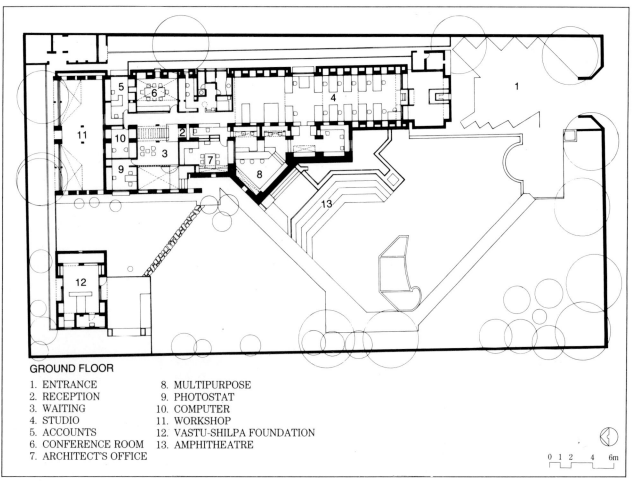

**GROUND FLOOR**

1. ENTRANCE
2. RECEPTION
3. WAITING
4. STUDIO
5. ACCOUNTS
6. CONFERENCE ROOM
7. ARCHITECT'S OFFICE
8. MULTIPURPOSE
9. PHOTOSTAT
10. COMPUTER
11. WORKSHOP
12. VASTU-SHILPA FOUNDATION
13. AMPHITHEATRE

0 1 2 4 6m

# Gandhi Labour Institute, Ahmedabad

## Architect: Balkrishna Doshi – Stein, Doshi and Bhalla

## Client: Gandhi Labour Institute

Consultants: C. H. Shah (structure), Stein, Doshi and Bhalla (services)

Contractor: H. K. Construction Company

Year of Completion: 1984

Area: 5600 m$^2$

This institutional complex is derived clearly from the architect's earlier experiments in his Sangath project. The atavistic language of vaults is explored here with pugnacious modernity. This building differs from its precedent, however, in its decidedly more urbanistic theme. Although motifs and traces of the paradise garden are worked into the environmental collage, fragmentary allusions to a townscape — plaza, courtyard, viaduct, street and stair — are the formal gestures of the composition.

The institute promotes research and training in labour welfare. Courses and seminars are short-term, and therefore there is no permanent student body and few staff. Only the Director lives on the campus. The complex has three distinct parts. The first, a two-storeyed academic block, has several seminar rooms, classrooms, a library, offices, lecture hall and an outdoor amphitheatre. The second, distinguished from the first by an angular skew, comprises the dining room and kitchen at the ground level with the Director's residence above. The students' dormitory is the third element, a tower in comparison to the other vaulted buildings. It is an elegantly proportioned mass surmounted by a slender white water tank.

The academic block is organized along a two-level vaulted circulation spine that serves as an exhibition gallery on the upper level. Specific functions such as the library and a public auditorium are defined by individual vaults that intersect the spine at right angles. A pair of these extensions containing offices and seminar rooms are linked by a third element to enclose a small court — a focal point for the overall complex. This urbanistic space flows out under the vault of the main circulation spine to the open plaza and amphitheatre beyond. A tartan structural grid incorporates corridors and inset terraces under small spans adjoining larger vaulted spaces.

1

1. Main stair, circulation spine
2. Roofscape
3. Amphitheatre court from director's terrace

*Overleaf*
4. Amphitheatre flanked by spinal vault
5. Principal internal court
6. Dormitory block
7. Director's residence
8. Dining hall opening to the garden

2

3

6

4

7

5

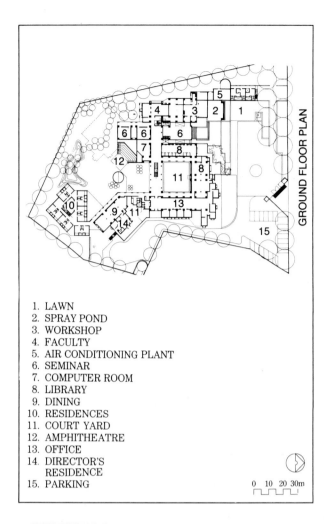

GROUND FLOOR PLAN

1. LAWN
2. SPRAY POND
3. WORKSHOP
4. FACULTY
5. AIR CONDITIONING PLANT
6. SEMINAR
7. COMPUTER ROOM
8. LIBRARY
9. DINING
10. RESIDENCES
11. COURT YARD
12. AMPHITHEATRE
13. OFFICE
14. DIRECTOR'S
    RESIDENCE
15. PARKING

0  10  20  30m

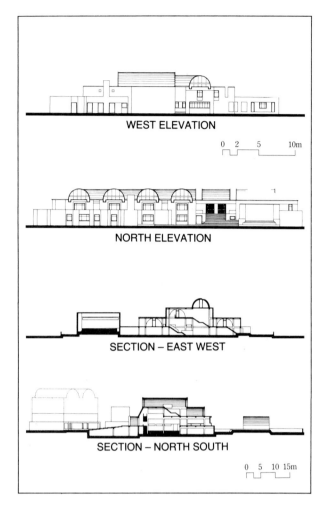

WEST ELEVATION

0  2   5        10m

NORTH ELEVATION

SECTION – EAST WEST

SECTION – NORTH SOUTH

0   5   10  15m

## Engineers India Limited, Offices, New Delhi

## Architect: Raj Rewal

## Client: Engineers India Limited

Consultants: Engineers India Limited (structure)
Contractors: Tarapore and Company
Year of Completion: 1983
Area: 18,216 m$^2$

The striking profile of this office building — a climatological innovation — is typical of the big-boned structural gestures favoured by this architect in his large urban commissions. The project forms the centrepiece of a massive district commercial centre for which the architect devised the master plan and architectural guidelines. The high-rise office block is exposed to the north and south on its long elevations. Each pair of floors forms a column-free truss that bridges two pairs of structural service cores. The skewed section of the building creates terraces on the north. The resulting overhangs protect the south-facing windows from direct exposure to the sun. Heat gain and the related air-conditioning costs are significantly reduced. Mechanical and electrical services and dismountable partitions are integrated with the exposed concrete structure. The building is clad with vertical slabs of yellow sandstone which are held in place with exposed metal bolts adding a decorative texture to the building.

1

2

3

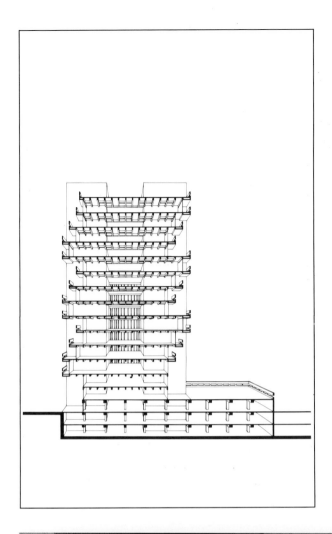

1. Stone facing
2. Sun breaking corbelling of the south facade
3. General view
4. Mezzanine, entrance hall

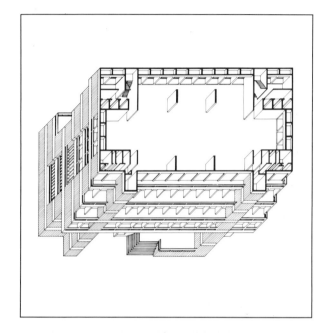

4                                                                                                                    193

National Institute of Immunology,
Staff Housing, New Delhi

Architect: Raj Rewal

Client: National Institute of
Immunology

Consultants: Vijay Rewal Associates (structure)

Contractor: Ahluwalia Contractors India Private
Limited

Year of Completion: Under construction

Area: Six housing clusters of varying sizes

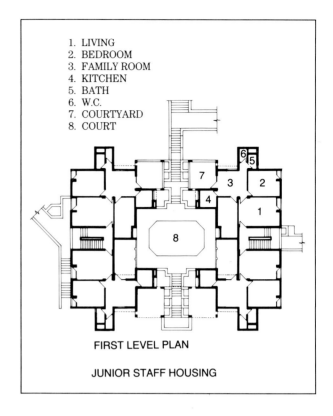

1. LIVING
2. BEDROOM
3. FAMILY ROOM
4. KITCHEN
5. BATH
6. W.C.
7. COURTYARD
8. COURT

FIRST LEVEL PLAN

JUNIOR STAFF HOUSING

The traditional desert architecture of
Rajasthan is an active inspiration in the design of
this institute. However, this complex is a more
sophisticated, subtle, and thoroughly modern
transformation of that morphology than this
architect's earlier experiment at the Asiad Village.
The project sits on the crest of a rocky ridge that
stretches through South Delhi with a commanding
view of the city and the Qutub Minar, a magnificent
twelfth century monument clad in red sandstone.
Three clusters of staff housing comprise the first
phase of this ongoing project — the first for
professors, the second for junior staff and the third
for scholars. Each cluster is organized around a
courtyard with its own distinctive character. The
three are interconnected with pedestrian paths that
follow contours of the land. Variations in the
courtyard designs give identity to each housing
type.

The 12-unit cluster for senior faculty is
entered along a diagonal axis, up a landscaped
slope. Ground-related units have garden extensions
and the upper units have access to large roof
terraces. The courtyard is a common entrance
garden. The junior staff housing is designed as a
monumental gateway to the complex; a rectangular
perimeter-block straddles a ceremonial staircase
leading up to the proposed auditorium. Care is
taken to maintain the privacy of individual units by
placing their entrances discretely to the side. The
scholars' housing is the most communal in spirit, a
ring of simple rooms enclosing an octagonal
amphitheatre set into the natural slope of the site
as it rises through the centre of the block. Effort
has been made to provide views of the rugged
landscape from housing units and their terraces
without sacrificing privacy.

The buildings are covered with crushed stone
plaster in a colourful deep red hue applied in
horizontal bands to reflect the pattern of the
structural frame and infill. A darker tone indicates
the structure and a lighter shade delineates
non-structural walls. Red sandstone pavers, dark
brown quartzite retaining walls and the burgundy
red soil set off the buildings with a warm glow that
recalls the old Islamic monuments nearby.

1. Scholars' residence, side elevation

*Overleaf*
2. Junior staff housing, internal court
3. Senior staff housing, internal court
4. Research facility under construction.
5. Scholars' residence from garden
6. Stair to main complex, junior staff housing

1

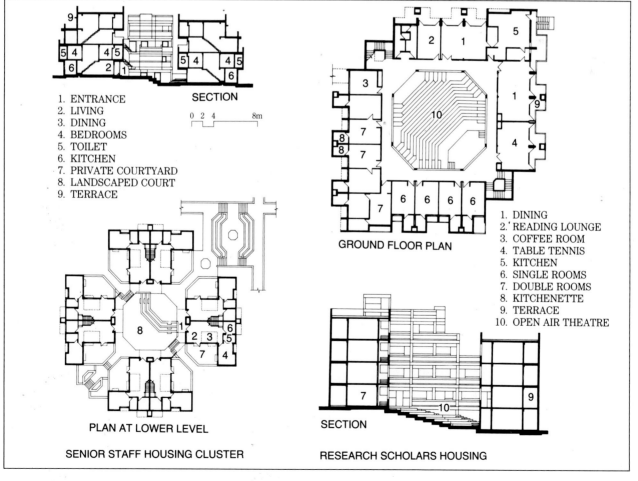

1. ENTRANCE
2. LIVING
3. DINING
4. BEDROOMS
5. TOILET
6. KITCHEN
7. PRIVATE COURTYARD
8. LANDSCAPED COURT
9. TERRACE

SECTION

0 2 4    8m

GROUND FLOOR PLAN

1. DINING
2. READING LOUNGE
3. COFFEE ROOM
4. TABLE TENNIS
5. KITCHEN
6. SINGLE ROOMS
7. DOUBLE ROOMS
8. KITCHENETTE
9. TERRACE
10. OPEN AIR THEATRE

PLAN AT LOWER LEVEL

SECTION

SENIOR STAFF HOUSING CLUSTER

RESEARCH SCHOLARS HOUSING

195

2

3

4

5

6

197

## Management Development Centre, Ahmedabad

### Architect: Anant D. Raje

### Client: Indian Institute of Management

Consultants: Sharad R. Shah (structure), Stein Doshi and Bhalla (services)

Contractor: Gannon Dunkerley and Company Limited

Year of Completion: 1982

Area: 4500 m$^2$

The honour of carrying on the work of a master was a difficult challenge well met in this prestigious academic building. The Management Development Centre is the last important element to be added to Louis Kahn's campus for the Indian Institute of Management left incomplete at his death in 1975. The architect has shown due respect for that powerful context by assiduously employing Kahn's brick vocabulary. But the building stands its own ground. It even takes Kahn's ideas on the intrinsic order of materials and light a step further. The play of light on fair-faced concrete is exploited originally, for example, in the elegant light shafts that pierce the central academic block of the complex. Taut planes of concrete — like stretched parchment — retain a narrow interface between the major spaces in the dark brick core of the building.

The complex is organized around a landscaped court. Two wings of guest rooms extend from the teaching block to complete the long sides of the quadrangle, the fourth side enclosed with a brick wall and a screen of trees. The symmetrical positioning of a pair of descending stairs in the concourse of the academic wing creates a large veranda-like terrace on the central axis of the block. Broad arches frame the view of the court. The comfortable, domestic scale of the quadrangle is established by manipulating its levels. Despite a masterful fidelity to the formal language of Kahn, this intimate, introverted composition is a refreshing exception to the overbearing weight and masculinity of the earlier campus buildings — a landmark in itself.

1. Interior court, junction of east wing and central block.
2. Guest room wing flanking upper and lower courts
3. Lower court
   *Overleaf*
4. Fair-face concrete light shaft, central block
5. Central block verandah

1

2

3

6

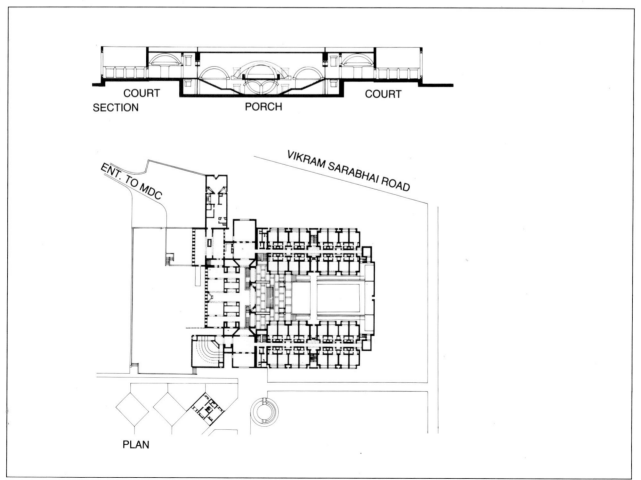

COURT
SECTION
PORCH
COURT

ENT. TO MDC

VIKRAM SARABHAI ROAD

PLAN

Farmers' Training Institute,
Palanpur, Gujarat

Architect: Anant D. Raje

Client: National Dairy Development
Board

Consultants: National Dairy Development Board
(structure and services)

Contractor: C. J. Kansara

Year of Completion: 1983

Area: 1100 m$^2$

This little campus is one in a network of rural training facilities operated by the National Dairy Development Board. It provides short-term instruction in applied agricultural technology to farmers and rural development workers in the important milk-producing region of northern Gujarat. The campus accommodates groups of 15 to 20 trainees at a time. Monk-like, they are encouraged in their studies by the self-contained isolation of the institute. Sleeping, eating, instruction, social activity and all daily functions revolve around the tiny cloister. This monastic analogy extends to the architecture in various respects. Spatial orientation is consistently inward looking. The curving sweep of the east wall decisively seals off the most public exposure of the building. One slips through a small gap to enter, only to arrive in a large windowless forecourt removed by several more courts and ante-chambers from the principal study and living spaces. The dining loggia and casual activity spaces look in on the central quadrangle. The two classrooms address a smaller, exclusive light court. In a manner reminiscent of monks' cells in European charterhouses, the L-shaped dormitories look in on semi-contained verandas in lieu of direct views of the rural landscape.

Construction is simple and powerful: rough-dressed stone bearing walls with clearly rendered slabs, arches and lintels in reinforced concrete. Floors and work areas in the kitchen and bathrooms are veneered with polished green sandstone. This empirical, stylistically timeless rendering of masonry brings coherence to the more obtuse logic behind the forms and organization of building elements. The austere image is softened by the intimacy of the composition and the relaxed manner in which it continues on its sloping

south-west exposure. All larger spaces, such as the charming dining hall, are open loggias which the client intends to enclose owing to the perennial infiltration of hot winds and dust.

1. General view
2. Entry to class rooms
3. Dining hall loggia

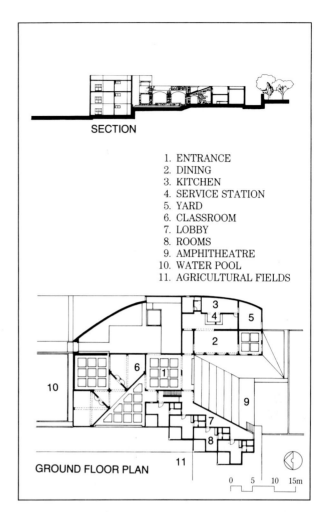

SECTION

1. ENTRANCE
2. DINING
3. KITCHEN
4. SERVICE STATION
5. YARD
6. CLASSROOM
7. LOBBY
8. ROOMS
9. AMPHITHEATRE
10. WATER POOL
11. AGRICULTURAL FIELDS

GROUND FLOOR PLAN

0  5  10  15m

3

## Indian Institute of Forest Management, Bhopal

## Architect: Anant D. Raje

## Client: Indian Institute of Forest Management

Consultants: Spectral Services Consultants Pvt. Ltd., New Delhi

Contractor:

Year of Completion: 1989

Area: 65 hectares

1. Library block
2. Exterior view, dormitory complex
3. Stone cladding detail
   *Overleaf*
4. Viaduct, detail
5. Viaduct linking library and teaching wing
6. Model, academic complex

Building on his smaller-scale institutional experiments including the diminutive Farmer's Training Institute at Palanpur, Gujarat, Anant Raje has conceived this large government project with a combination of romanticism and monumentality unprecedented in recent Indian architecture. The architect's deep veneration for Louis Kahn is undisguised, but he has allowed himself exceptional licence to distort and enrich Kahn's idiom in comparison to his Management Development Centre. Contemporary images are secondary in their influence of the design; the primary inspiration is historical. Just as Louis Kahn turned to Roman ruins such as Hadrian's Villa as a source of architectural forms and relationships, this campus derives its complex assemblage of spaces, elements and arched masonry from classical Deccan architecture. The enigmatic majesty of the ruined palace of Mandu — as captured in the architect's sketches — is translated into contemporary structures more delicate in mass and proportion, but characterized all the more by that gaunt and haunted quality of a ruin. The plan is a palimpsest: a formal base order half effaced by an overlay of autonomous, sometimes colliding geometries, like successive archaeological deposits on a single site. Bordering the complex is a linear reflecting pool that serves as the datum for the composition. A series of monumental loggia make the transition from this water body and its esoteric formalism to the more mundane complex of office and teaching blocks behind. Structural order is determined by functional and symbolic criteria. The plan is resolved into distinct components, some of which are repeated, as in the faculty offices, or skewed off the base grid and distinguished by their own geometry. The dense congregation of structures creates a romantic sequence of semi-enclosed and open-to-sky spaces intimate enough in scale to be a useful, sun-protected extension of the architectural environment.

1

2

3

4

5

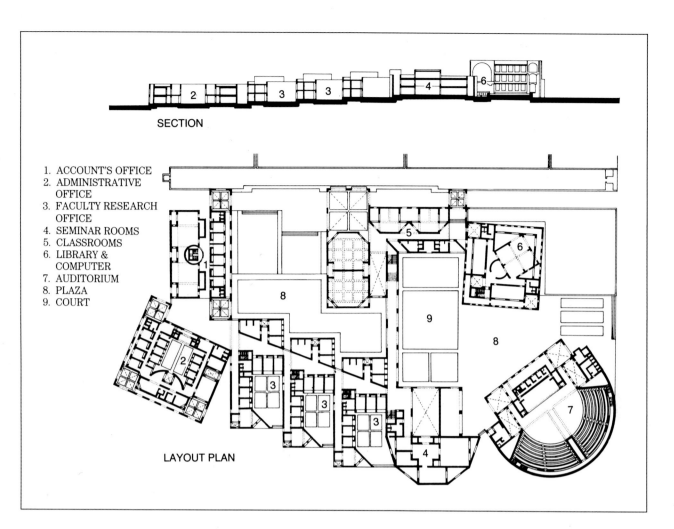

SECTION

1. ACCOUNT'S OFFICE
2. ADMINISTRATIVE
   OFFICE
3. FACULTY RESEARCH
   OFFICE
4. SEMINAR ROOMS
5. CLASSROOMS
6. LIBRARY &
   COMPUTER
7. AUDITORIUM
8. PLAZA
9. COURT

LAYOUT PLAN

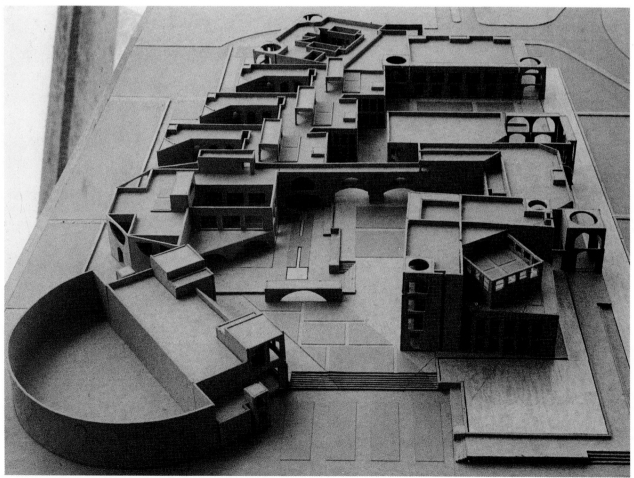

## Sainik Guest House, Bhopal

### Architect: Sen Kapadia

### Client: Directorate of Sainik Welfare, Madhya Pradesh

Consultants: Pravin Gala (structure)

Contractor: Ganshay H. Mirchandani

Year of Completion: 1986

Area: 550 m$^2$

As an experiment in architectural perception the architect avoided the use of elevation drawings in the process of designing this building. The third dimension was visualized exclusively through axonometric drawings with graphically arresting results. The building has a simple programme: commercial space and several storeys of dormitories and private guest rooms above. These are intended for the short-term accommodation of ex-military servicemen passing through the city. The various space types are organized around a vertical circulation core with wings stretching out on two sides. The core is crowned with a service penthouse and expressive skylight shafts. The two wings are highly unusual in section and plan. To increase exposure to the north and overshadow the south side of the building each successive level is skewed a few degrees further south in a fan-like manner with the central core as the pivotal point. Windows on either side of each wing make rooms bright and airy. As a result of the angular rotation in plan, some of the rooms on the upper floors are transformed into trapezoids; a quirky quality of space. However, segments of some of the balconies with their skewing *chajjas* (overhangs) have become so tight that they are impossible to enter.

1

2

3

1. Fanning terraces, north facade
2. Southern facade
3. Dormitory
4. General view

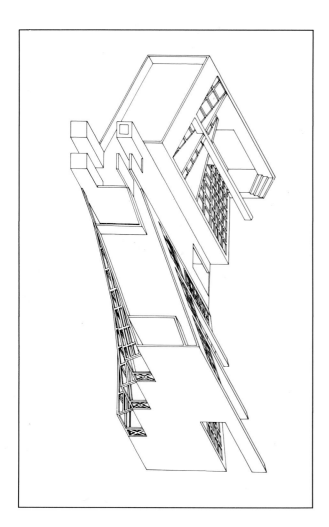

SAINIK GUEST HOUSE

4

## Food Crafts Institute, Students' Hostels, Bhopal

### Architect: Sen Kapadia

### Client: The Food Crafts Institute

Contractor: Ravi Construction Company

Year of Completion: 1985

Area: 1067 m$^2$

Curvilinear form and trendy colours — blue for boys and pink for girls — set off these two buildings in contrast to the surrounding drab, middle-income housing. Similar in design method to the architect's Sainik Guest House and other projects of the same period, the eccentricities of these institutional hostels result from a re-interpretation of the standard building type through alternative drawing techniques. The hostels are planned as two parallel and relatively identical wings oriented north-south. The southern facades are partially bermed under earth to reduce direct exposure to the sun. A single-loaded corridor on two levels opens to the north like a veranda. The sensual integration of buildings and landscape lends the composition a sculptural quality that is somewhat bizarre despite its climatological rationale. Unfortunately, the pristine purism of the forms relies for its effect on a high standard of maintenance because of the hot, dusty climate and the characteristic irreverence of the adolescent student occupants. The cement culverts that pierce students' rooms on the lower tier of each block are difficult to clean, attracting dirt and refuse. The berms themselves are crumbling because of the absence of grass.

1. North facade.
2. Undulating southern facade
3. Earth berm with ventilation shafts

1

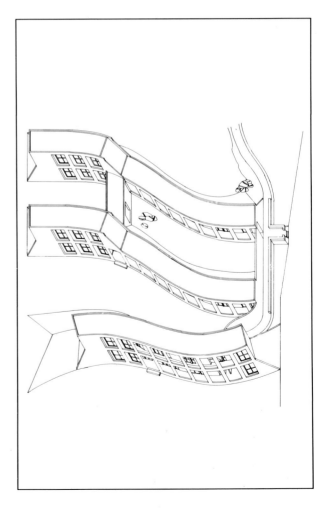

# School for Spastic Children, New Delhi

## Architect: Romi Khosla — Grup India Limited, New Delhi

## Client: The Spastics Society of Northern India

Consultant: Semac Private Limited

Contractor: Alhuwalia Contractors India Private Limited

Year of Completion: 1985

Area: 558 m$^2$

The special constraints in the programme for this school building encouraged the architect to exploit some unconventional form sources for his design. The mother's womb and its architectural analogy in the rock-cut cave temples of ancient India, provided the formal idea for a protective, internalized environment of soft shapes and surfaces that an intelligent, but physically handicapped child could safely explore. The sweeping curves — ramps and balconies of the internal facade with their piped railings painted fire-engine red — give a dynamism to the building suggestive of a grandstand at a hippodrome. This is a contrast to the austere fortress-like exterior intended to project an impression of security for the special environment within. The dichotomy is exaggerated — ambiguously, however — by the semi-completed state of the building which has left both internal and external facades exposed. The external wall is perforated at intervals by large sculpted openings in which all fenestration is concentrated. The over-sized scallop shape of these openings is highly evocative but irrational because of the materials employed. The red brick wall is seemingly garnished with the exposed concrete structure that supports it. The disappointing lack of technical rigour undermines the success of the architect's intriguing iconographic gestures.

1. Classroom
2. Sweeping curves of interior terraces and ramp
3. External facade, fenestration detail

*Overleaf*
4. Fenestration, detail
5. Study model
6. Interior facade
7. Ramp detail

1

2

4

6

5

## Chakravarty Residence, New Delhi

### Architect: Romi Khosla — Grup India Limited, New Delhi

### Client: Professor Chakravarty

Year of Completion: 1975

Area: 60 m$^2$

The source image for the Chakravarty residence is the naive representation of a house with a sloped roof and an oversized chimney that a child might draw. The designer has acknowledged his debt, in this regard, to Robert Venturi and his ideas on the symbolic intentions of architecture. But the undiscerning interpretation of what must be considered an American or European *gestalt* of house suggests that the visual inspiration of Venturi's actual projects, such as his mother's house at Chestnut Hill, Pennsylvania, has overruled the wider implications of his ideas as applied by his Indian admirer. The Chakravarty house is a small brick building dominated by the incongruous form of its large gabled roof. It contains two ordinary rooms, with kitchen, bathroom, and a small terrace at the rear. A quirky chimney form that surmounts the whole is purely vestigal.

This odd little house might have been conceived of more naturally in the salubrious cool of the Himalayan foothills at Simla, a pukka sahib's cottage. It lies, however, in the hot plains of the Yamuna on a narrow site squeezed between the crass suburban bungalows of South Delhi. This irony is apparent in the slightly absurd caricature that the building presents as its image; an inference to the neo-colonial reveries that still pervade the lifestyle and ideals of middle-class India.

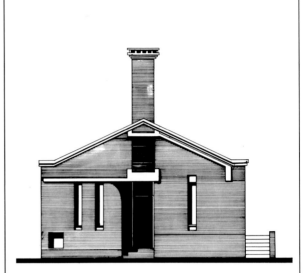

SIDE ELEVATION

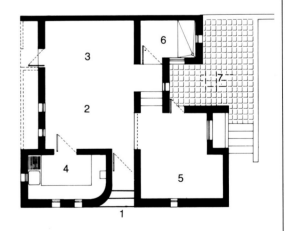

1. ENTRANCE
2. DINING
3. LIVING
4. KITCHEN
5. BEDROOM
6. TOILET
7. COURTYARD

1. Decorative brick work, detail
2. General view from rear garden

1

2                                                                                                    217

# Roman Catholic Church of Gaekwad-ni-Haveli, Ahmedabad

## Architect: Leo Pereira

## Client: Catholic Church, Ahmedabad

Consultant: J.P. Shah (structure)

Contractor: Hasmukh Construction Company

Year of Completion: 1979

Area: 157 m$^2$

This modest Christian sanctuary stands proudly but discreetly in a dense old quarter of Ahmedabad. Surrounding neighbourhoods are predominantly Muslim. A special challenge of this low-budged commission came from the necessity to build on the congregation's only available real estate, a crowded burial plot. Some of the tombs, and the distinctive sanctity of the place have been incorporated in the building. The chapel is separated from a busy street by a level change of half a storey negotiated through a bower of flowering vines. This leads through a strip of wild garden to a forecourt bordered by the church and the superintendent's dwelling. A delicate pergola screens this outdoor room from the sun allowing it to serve as an extra space for overflowing gatherings during major ceremonies. The nave is a long, low shaft of space contained between windowless masonry walls, plastered with a skewing open-to sky apse beyond the glazed north wall of the altar. The architect has made a curious fulcrum for the design out of a pair of existing tombs in the forecourt. The building is generated by purist aesthetics and an interest in the architectural manipulation of daylight; tendencies cultivated by the architect during a period of post-graduate training in Denmark. The chapel is rendered with a spartan simplicity that compares confidently with the sacred architecture of Utzon and Aalto while remaining a suitably tropical building.

1. Stair to forecourt with tomb.
2. View of church and garden from street.

1

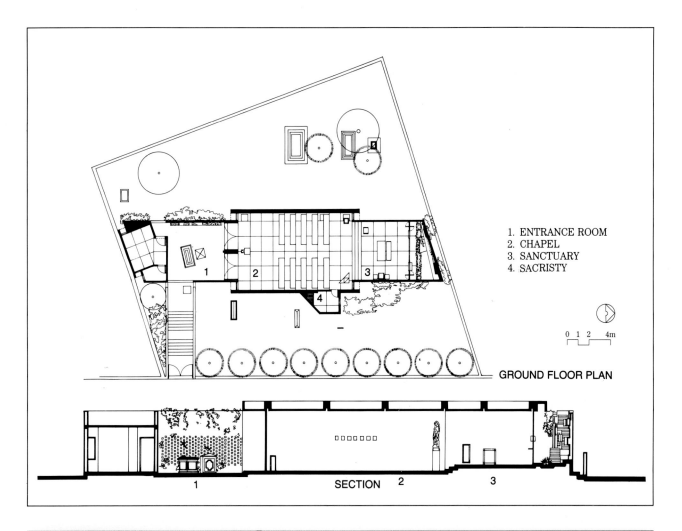

1. ENTRANCE ROOM
2. CHAPEL
3. SANCTUARY
4. SACRISTY

GROUND FLOOR PLAN

0 1 2    4m

SECTION    1    2    3

## Architect's Own House, Ahmedabad

## Architect: Leo Pereira

Consultant: J.P. Shah (structure)

Contractor: Bricon Construction Company

Year of Completion: 1983

Area: 90 m$^2$

The house that Leo Pereira had designed for himself and his family is his quintessential work to date. The dining room, where important family exchanges takes place, is the nucleus of both the house and garden, and is directly linked to both through recessed verandas on both the east and west exposures. Each chamber of the interior emerges into the central dining space, and a light-bathed stairwell rises from this point to the single upper story chamber and adjoining roof terrace directly above. A water tank crowns the stepped-back volume of the house; a bi-axially symmetric composition that gives the impression of a puckish little ziggurat.

The chaste exterior of the house is surfaced in whitewashed plaster that contrasts smartly with exposed horizontal elements of the concrete structure. Inside, polished green sandstone distinguishes all floors as well as the built-in shelving, seating and work stations. The interiors are enchanted spaces where the fierce Indian sun is permitted to seep in only by various discrete modes of indirection. Window apertures are characteristically arranged in low horizontal bands that prevent views of the sun and sky whilst framing magic glimpses of garden greenery. Deft level changes in both floor and ceiling and the projection of wall planes above the chest-high window lintels serve to animate the interior volume to delightful effect.

GROUND FLOOR PLAN

1. ENTRANCE
2. LIVING
3. DINING
4. KITCHEN
5. MASTER BEDROOM
6. STUDY/GUEST ROOM
7. BATH
8. VERANDAH
9. STORE
10. SERVANT'S ROOM
11. SERVANT'S TOILET

0    10    20m

1

2

1. Dining room
2. Living room
3. Fenestration detail
4. Garden facade

3

4

$\frac{4}{95}^5$   $\frac{10}{20}^5 (95)$